Your Towns and Cities in

Folkestone

in the Great War

Your Towns and Cities in the Great War

Folkestone

in the Great War

by Stephen Wynn

First published in Great Britain in 2017 by
PEN & SWORD MILITARY
an imprint of
Pen and Sword Books Ltd
47 Church Street
Barnsley
South Yorkshire S70 2AS

ISBN 978 1 47382 792 9

Printed and bound in England
by CPI Group (UK) Ltd, Croydon, CR0 4YY

Pen & Sword Books Ltd incorporates the imprints of
Pen & Sword Archaeology, Atlas, Aviation, Battleground, Discovery,
Family History, History, Maritime, Military, Naval, Politics, Railways,
Select, Social History, Transport, True Crime, and Claymore Press,
Frontline Books, Leo Cooper, Praetorian Press, Remember When,
Seaforth Publishing and Wharncliffe.

For a complete list of Pen and Sword titles please contact
Pen and Sword Books Limited
47 Church Street, Barnsley, South Yorkshire, S70 2AS, England
E-mail: enquiries@pen-and-sword.co.uk
Website: www.pen-and-sword.co.uk

Contents

Author's biography

Stephen is a happily retired police officer having served with Essex Police as a constable for thirty years between 1983 and 2013. He is married to Tanya who is also his best friend.

Both his sons, Luke and Ross, were members of the armed forces, collectively serving five tours of Afghanistan between 2008 and 2013. Both were injured on their first tour. This led to his first book *Two Sons in a Warzone – Afghanistan: The True Story of a Fathers Conflict*, published in October 2010.

He has a teenage daughter, Aimee, who currently attends secondary school.

Both of his grandfathers served in and survived the First World War, one with the Royal Irish Rifles, the other in the Mercantile Navy. His father was a member of the Royal Army Ordnance Corps during the Second World War.

Stephen collaborated with one of his writing partners, Ken Porter, on a previous book published in August 2012, *'German POW Camp 266 – Langdon Hills*, which spent six weeks as the number one best-selling book in Waterstones, Basildon between March and April 2013. Steve and Ken collaborated on a further four books in the 'Towns & Cities in the Great War' series by Pen & Sword. Stephen has also written other titles for the same series of books.

Stephen has also cowritten three crime thrillers which were published between 2010 and 2012; they centre around a fictional detective named Terry Danvers.

When he is not writing, Tanya and he enjoy the simplicity of walking their four German Shepherd dogs early each morning when most sensible people are still fast asleep in their beds.

CHAPTER ONE

A Brief History of Folkestone and the Outbreak of War

Folkestone became one of the most important British towns of the First World War, mainly due to the fact that it was in the part of the country nearest to the fighting in Europe and the shortest crossing point between England and France. The shorter time that a boat was in the water carrying thousands of men and nurses across the English Channel, the less opportunity there would be for a German U-Boat to attack it.

Before the war Folkestone had been a well established and much loved holiday destination for thousands of people searching for a brief escape from the drudgery and harshness of everyday life, especially those from London; the air which they breathed for most of their lives was far from clean and fresh. It was difficult to find a more enjoyable and more agreeable location to visit than Folkestone, with its unpolluted air, its gentle sea breezes, its sun-kissed beaches and its tastefully decorated seafront promenades.

People could take a leisurely stroll along the Leas, taking in the simple but breathtaking views as they looked out to sea. The harbour was always a hive of activity with fishing boats coming and going with the tides. The beach area was awash with traders trying their best to make a few pennies from the hordes of holidaymakers who poured into the town nearly every day, especially through the summer months and at weekends.

For the more affluent holidaymaker, there was the opportunity to catch a passenger ferry across to France for a day trip or a longer stay. With the outbreak of the war in August 1914, and for the next four and a half years, Folkestone wouldn't quite be the same place.

When the possibility of war became a reality, Folkestone suddenly had to address an issue which had never been a problem before. This was about the German and Austrian residents who lived in Folkestone, most of whom either worked 'in service' or in one of the town's hotels.

The Illustrated War News of 12 August 1914 carried an article, with a photograph, about German reservists who had been detained at Folkestone Harbour after they were prevented from catching a ship to Flushing in Holland, from where they would have made their way back to Germany, having either been called up by the German authorities, or wanting voluntarily to enlist in the German Army.

A total of 285 German men of enlistment age were detained on the grounds that the time period allowed for enemy aliens to leave Great Britain had expired. It was suggested that most of the men did not

German Reservists being marched off to Shorncliffe Barracks
(The Illustrated War News)

appear too perturbed when told by British military authorities that they were not going to be allowed to return to Germany and instead were going to be detained. They were marched off, through the town, to Shorncliffe Barracks. It was a warm sunny day and the large group of Germans were flanked on either side by British Tommys, with their Lee Enfield rifles slung across their left shoulders, bayonets fixed. None of the German Reservists were carrying any luggage or any other items of private property, this was placed in motor vehicles and driven to Shorncliffe camp to be collected on their arrival. The newspaper article included a statement which had been issued by the Home Secretary on 10 August 1914 to address the issue of enemy aliens:

> *A considerable number of Germans, chiefly reservists, have been arrested in various parts of the country. This has been done as a precautionary measure and in accordance with what is usual in the early stages of a war, but it is not likely that the detention of most of the prisoners will be prolonged. The great majority of Germans remaining in this country are peaceful and innocent persons from whom no danger is to be feared.*

The German Reservists detained at Folkestone Harbour eventually ended up being prevented from leaving the country at Christ's Hospital School in Horsham which, by all accounts, provided excellent accommodation.

CHAPTER TWO

1914 – Starting Out

In the eyes of some, the war was just going to be a bit of fun that would all be over by Christmas, and that all the British would have to do would be to turn up, shout the word 'Boo' very loudly towards the nasty, cowardly Hun, and they would all just simply disappear as quickly as they had arrived. The belief was that everybody would be back home in time to share the festive holidays with their families, with tales of derring-do to talk about in front of a nice hot fire.

That's not quite how it turned out. According to figures provided by the Commonwealth War Graves website; in the first four weeks of the war, between 4 and 31 August, British and Commonwealth forces had already lost 2,841 men killed. That is an average of 101 men killed every day. September didn't get any better, in fact it became worse, with more than double the number killed, 6,891 to be precise, the daily average rising to 230. By October it was getting out of hand, as 11,343 more men lost their lives; a daily average of 366. Losses for November were still worse, but only just. A total of 11,496 lives were extinguished, snuffed out, gone for evermore, men destined never to return home to their loved ones.

December was one of the better months as far as British and Commonwealth deaths went, but it was still bad. The records show that 5,045 men were killed, or an average of 163 men a day. So for the first five months of the war, what was originally going to be just an easy jaunt across the English Channel, so that the nasty old Hun could be given a bloody nose and put in his place once and for all, resulted in the deaths of 37,616 British and Commonwealth soldiers, or 251 each day for the first 150 days of the war. By 1915, people were viewing the war in a totally different light.

The war was only a week old when Folkestone was declared a prohibited military area and all those who were not British subjects, of whatever nationality, had to officially register with the local police and provide a satisfactory reason as to why they should be allowed to remain in the town. During the first week of the restriction more than 1,000 foreign aliens applied to be allowed to remain in Folkestone.

With the outbreak of war, the residents of Folkestone noticed an almost immediate change in the town. Although the sun and blue skies hadn't left, the holidaymakers had, and they wouldn't be coming back anytime soon. The restaurants, cafés, hotels, guesthouses, general traders, taxis and buses, suddenly had little or no trade. It was a stark awakening of just how wide-sweeping the effects of war could be, and how quickly they could be felt.

The local weekly newspaper, *The Folkestone, Hythe, Sandgate & Cheriton Herald*, dated Saturday, 8 August 1914, carried a report about stranded holidaymakers on the Continent caught out by the outbreak of war. It was a time of year when thousands of the more affluent members of British society regularly took holidays in Europe, to such countries as France, Switzerland, Holland and Germany. While a large proportion of these made it safely home, there were hundreds more who found themselves stranded. There was a rush to get to ports such as Calais, Boulogne, Ostend or Flushing to catch crowded boats back to England. Most of these boats made their way to Folkestone. Extra trains were needed to cope with the rush of passengers who were arriving at the harbour.

The issue of stranded holidaymakers wasn't just in one direction. There were reports of French people unable to leave and similar difficulties befell German tourists. Some caught trains to London, while others decided to stay in Folkestone. Not surprisingly in the circumstances, they found it hard to obtain lodgings.

The last few days of peace saw an almost unbelievable amount of traffic coming into and leaving Folkestone as the buildup to the outbreak of war continued. The Flushing boat on Sunday (2 August) was four hours late and had nearly 1,000 passengers on board, most of whom were returning British holidaymakers. The cause of the delay was the large amount of people who wanted to get on the boat, along with the extra time it took to get all of the extra luggage on as well.

That same day, the turbine steamer the *Victoria* left Boulogne with 1,000 passengers on board, at noon, but had to leave behind a further 400 on the quayside for whom they simply had no room. Those left behind were found space on the SS *Onward,* which had been sent from Dover to pick them up.

On the eve of the war an altercation took place at Folkestone Harbour between a party of Frenchmen and a group of Germans, who were waiting at the same time to catch vessels back to Boulogne and Flushing. Once each of the groups realised the nationality of the other, 'it all kicked off' in 'a rare old fashion'. However, no real damage was done by either side, who were split up by railway officials and police officers.

The early part of the week saw a lot of outward bound traffic leaving from Folkestone Harbour. This included Austrian Reservists on their way back home to join their Regiments, and French Reservists who had travelled by train from Charing Cross in London to Folkestone on the Sunday and the Monday. The scenes at the London Terminus were touching as young Frenchmen, some looking more akin to school boys rather than young men, who were about to go off to war, bade farewell to their loved ones. On their arrival at Folkestone they were in high spirits. Once at the harbour they were singing and cheering and waving small tricolour flags. There were crowds of well-wishers on the Pier to see them off. Once on board, the young soldiers gathered together and after removing their hats sang the *Marseillaise.* Many of the onlookers tried their best to join in but with French not being their mother tongue it was not possible. Many of the men in the crowd raised their hats and contented themselves with cries of 'Vive L'Angleterre!' and 'Vive La France!' As the vessel made its way slowly out of the harbour, there were loud cheers and the waving of handkerchiefs. The same scenes were repeated the following day in both morning and afternoon as more Frenchmen left to go off to war.

Members of the British Royal Naval Reserve had been met with a similar enthusiastic send-off on the Sunday when they gathered in the harbour to board their allocated vessels.

On Wednesday, 5 August, and with the war only one day old, the military authorities in Folkestone began enforcing Section 15 of the Army Act. Once they had obtained a signed authorisation from a local magistrate, they could compulsorily purchase any animals and vehicles that they might require.

Captain H. Eyre, the District Remount Officer, having acquired the necessary signature from Councillor W.J. Harrison, went about his business and at once attended the yard of Mr Frank Funnell which was in Sandgate Road at the East Kent Hotel. After looking over his horses, Captain Eyre and his team purchased sixty of them, paying between £50 and £70 for each animal. Other horse owners in the town were also visited by Captain Eyre and his team. A number of local motor vehicles were also purchased during the course of the day.

As an aside, a Captain H.W. Eyre was killed in action while serving in France, on 29 July 1916, with the 2nd/6th Battalion, Gloucestershire Regiment and is buried in the Pas-de-Calais region of France.

It wasn't only horses and motor vehicles which Folkestone residents provided for the war effort. Members of the Folkestone and District Homing Pigeon Society offered their birds to the Secretary of State for War, for the conveying of messages on the Western Front and other locations where their use might prove beneficial to the war effort. Their offer was gratefully accepted. This message system went on to become an integral part of the lines of communications used on the Western Front between units in the trenches.

The Folkestone Society held their 4th Young Bird race on the Saturday before the outbreak of the war and demonstrated how far some of these birds could fly; the birds flew a distance of 101 miles. The first bird home, owned by a Mr Green, flew at an average of 1,071 yards a minute.

On Wednesday, 5 August, 'D' Company (Folkestone) of the 1st/4th Battalion, East Kent (the Buffs) Regiment, which was a Territorial Unit, left Junction railway station in the afternoon on route for their allotted position in the scheme of mobilization for home defence. It was a bittersweet send-off; enthusiastic and joyous on the one hand, sadness and worry on the other.

Though the parting scenes at the Drill Hall were a new experience to many, there were those among the watching onlookers who remembered the departure of the Volunteers during the time of the Boer War, under the leadership of Captain (now Lieutenant Colonel) Graham Gosling. It was noted that the Volunteers of the Boer War departed full of confidence, taking items with them that had nothing to do with war, such as musical instruments.

The latter-day Buffs left sounding jolly and light hearted, but in a more business-like manner, maybe because their wives, children and mothers were all there to see them off, which resulted in both sides struggling to cope with their emotions.

'D' Company left the Drill Hall amid cheers and applause and slowly marched off to the Junction station. On the way they were met with great enthusiasm from large crowds gathering along the route. Captain Arthur Atkinson was in command and was in company with his fellow officers, Lieutenant H.G. Williams, and Lieutenant W. Williams. A machine gun section, under Sergeants Gosby and Newman, also left from Junction station later in the afternoon.

Among those who left from the Drill Hall to the railway station with the men was Reverend John Charles Carlile, who in 1920 wrote the book *Folkestone During the War (1914-1919) a Record of the Town's Life and Work*.

When the soldiers arrived at Junction station, they were met by an even larger crowd, who were also there to give them an enthusiastic send-off. The Town Crier was present, looking resplendent in his scarlet uniform, with Bell in hand. Without too much ceremony the men got on the train, stowed their kit bags and equipment, and hung out of the windows, shouting and waving as the train slowly pulled out of the station, to the accompaniment of more loud cheers.

From there they went to Canterbury as part of the Home Counties Division, where they remained until 29 October 1914 when they left for India on board the HM Transport *Dongola*, about 180 Folkestone men in total.

On Friday, 7 August 1914, the Buffs were followed out of Folkestone by men of the local Territorial Royal Field Artillery Unit. In particular, men of the 2nd Kent Battery of the 3rd Home Counties (Cinque Ports) Brigade. They had arrived home from their summer camp on the Wednesday evening, 5 August, disembarking at

Shorncliffe railway station. Since then other men had enlisted and the Battery was at full strength by the time of its departure.

Just like the Buffs they had set off from the Drill Hall at Shellons Street and marched up to the Junction railway station amidst enthusiastic support, before leaving for their destination by train. The men were under the command of Major W.B. Kennett, whose fellow officers included Captain S. Lambert Weston, Lieutenant S.A. Wise, Lieutenant V.G. Loyd and Lieutenant Boyd.

The town's restaurants and hotels had all been affected to a certain degree by the departure of so many French and Germans who had been waiters, chefs and workers in many of Folkestone's biggest and best loved hotels and restaurants. The blow of losing so many staff was ironically softened somewhat by its timing, the London season had just come to an end, meaning that many of the staff would be looking for jobs. Folkestone would be one of the first towns they would look to for new employment.

Food, or rather the perceived lack of it, had become a real issue in Folkestone, as it had led to many people panic buying, especially among the more affluent of the community. On the very day that war was announced, most of the town's provision shops were besieged by people wishing to place unusually large orders, causing several of them to have to close. But thankfully by Thursday, the 6th, common sense had prevailed. People had realised that there were not going to be any sudden food shortages, and with all such apprehensions largely dispelled, a calm returned to proceedings.

Now the war had begun, people still took in the sea views, but they were now looking through different eyes. No longer were they thinking about the wonder of the sea and the escapism it delivered, now it was fear and a belief that soon the Germans would be coming across the English Channel, not as holidaymakers, but an invading army.

On 20 August Belgian refugees started arriving. They arrived by the boat load, or rather in nearly any type of vessel that would stay afloat long enough to get them across the Channel, so desperate were they to escape the tentacles of an ever advancing German Army.

Possibly because of the restrictions of the Defence of the Realm Act (DORA), which provided both the Government and the military with some far reaching wartime powers, the press both locally and nationally were not able freely to print whatever they wanted. So the arrival of the Belgians in Folkestone was not reported for more than a week. One of the initial issues with the arrival of the refugees was a lack of organisation and logistics. This wasn't a British Government sanctioned evacuation, this was an instinctive act of survival by individuals who were in fear of their lives and those of their families. Because of this when they arrived in Folkestone they were utterly reliant on the good will and kindness of their unsuspecting hosts. Some had been travelling for days, on foot to start with, then by train and then on the final leg of their journey by boat across the English Channel, to an uncertain future, with no idea how long they would stay or when they would return to their homeland. They had arrived in their thousands within just a matter of days and each and every one of them needed accommodation and food.

In late August 1914 the people of Folkestone started putting the refugee situation on a more official footing by forming the Folkestone Refugee Relief Committee. Some of the town's most important and influential individuals were part of it, including the Mayor, Stephen Penfold, who was later knighted for his services to Folkestone and the war effort. The Deputy Mayor, Mr Alderman Spurgeon, was also on the board. The refugee situation was assisted by a Belgian Relief Fund which had been instigated and set up by elements of the press. Newspapers, both local and national, were involved which helped the refugee situation greatly, by financing much-needed food and clothing.

Everybody pulled together, from shopkeepers to hotel owners. The local churches played a particularly active part, not only by organising food collections but giving up their church halls for sleeping accommodation. Appeals were made for bedding and clothing. Logistically the Belgian refugee situation became such a massive issue the Government had to become involved, as it quickly became apparent that Folkestone on her own was not going to be able to cope. Advisors were sent from London to advise and coordinate matters in relation to the almost continuous stream of refugees pouring in to the town.

It was just not possible for Folkestone to carry on taking in all of the refugees arriving in the town. Other towns across the south coast had to take their share of the refugees as well. Besides the Belgian refugees, wounded Belgian soldiers also found Folkestone to be their first port of call when they were sent to England for hospital treatment.

In the first month of the war an estimated 18,000 refugees arrived at Folkestone Harbour from Belgium; eventually over 100,000 would make good their escape from their war-torn country, including musicians and renowned artists, such as Fredo Franzoni, and members of the Belgian Royal family. The latter were put up in the rather sumptuous surroundings of the Grand Hotel, which sits high up on the Leas.

It was the middle of October before the daily arrivals of refugees at Folkestone Harbour stopped. Once the dust had settled, around 15,000 of them remained in the town, which required a continuing commitment from members of the community. All of the refugees needed somewhere to live and all had to be fed.

The first wounded British soldiers arrived back home in England at Folkestone on the evening of 27 August 1914. They had arrived from the ports of Boulogne and Rouen in France after the retreat from the Battle of Mons.

Two Scottish Highlanders on their way back to England. What would young and scared German soldiers have thought when they saw large numbers of men running towards them, rifle in hand with bayonet attached, wearing what they would have understandably thought were skirts?

A wounded Scottish Highlander being helped at Boulogne. In both pictures it is noticeable how cheery all of the men appear to be. But then they had just arrived home after taking part in the Battle of Mons where they had seen at first hand the bloody brutality of war, where some of their friends and colleagues had not been as fortunate as they had, so they must have felt great relief at having escaped that living hell. Their arrival was another example of just how real the war was, as if anybody actually needed reminding of that fact.

In the early days of November 1914, the headquarters of the Belgian Refugees, which was situated at the Old Harvey Grammar School in Foord Road, saw a big increase in the number of meals that it was having to serve, owing to the arrival of Belgian soldiers. Another reason for the increase was that destitute refugees had started to arrive from the cities of Ghent and Bruges. They had managed to escape the

Belgian refugees at Folkestone (Permission John Lander)

A group of Belgian refugees in Folkestone (Permission John Lander)

advance of the German Army by making their way to Holland. Once there, they were finding passage on ships out of Flushing that were heading to England.

In November 1914 the Folkestone Volunteer Corps was formed at a meeting in the Town Hall. The Executive Committee was made up of Colonel G. Power, Mr F. Scarborough, Mr A.R. Bowles, Mr Henry Brooke, Mr G.W. Haines, who was also appointed the Honorary Secretary, Colonel Owen, who was the appointed Military Adviser, and Major H.R.J. Williams who was appointed as the corps officer commanding. The drill sergeant was Sergeant Major Vickery, Royal Engineers, who had the task of putting the men through their drills.

Initially the men were viewed by some as a bit of a laughing stock. This was mainly because not only did the men have to provide their own uniforms but they even had to drill with wooden, make-believe rifles, which naturally didn't do their credibility any good in the eyes of the public. Even though they were officially recognised by the War Office, it wouldn't be until 1918 that they were supplied with rifles, tin hats, bayonets and gas masks. This delay was somewhat strange, given their purpose for being in existence, which was to defend their country in the event of a German invasion.

To give themselves a professional veneer, the Corps was affiliated to the Central Association of Volunteer Training Corps. To become professional their members had to be prepared to work extremely hard, so despite holding down a day job they had to attend at the town's Drill Hall two evenings a week for drill training and other instruction.

In January 1915 the Corps had 316 members. Of this number 239 were over the age of 38 and seventy-seven of them were under the age of 38.

Members of the Corps were not subjected to military discipline and, despite the country being involved in a war, they were free to leave any time they wanted to, only having to give two weeks' notice. This did seem somewhat at odds with the situation the country was in at the time, and was rightly addressed. This clause came from the Volunteer Act 1863 and, although by 1914 it was more than fifty years old, it had never been repealed. When in early 1916 conscription came into being, Military Service Tribunals, which had to deal with the men who were looking to be exempt from military service, could order these men to join their local Volunteer Training Corps. This meant that the two Acts were at loggerheads with each other and something needed to be done to rectify the matter. This came in the shape of the Volunteer Act 1916 which obliged men of the Volunteer Training Corps to remain members for the duration of the war.

Nationally the Volunteer Training Corps was an impressive body of men and an effective force to have in place should the threat of an invasion by Germany ever have become a reality. They were supported by some very powerful

Proficiency Badge of the Volunteer Training Corps

Volunteer Training Corps Uniforms

PRIVATE.
Original Pattern.)

OFFICER.
(The Rank Mark is that of a Company Commander.)

PRIVATE.
(Permissible Alternative Style.)

UNIFORMS.

individuals of the time. Lord Desborough became the President of the Central Association of Volunteer Training Corps, and Sir Garrett O'Moore Creagh VC became its Military Adviser. By 1918 their numbers stood at 285,000. What wasn't so impressive was that of this number, some 110,000 had been instructed to join the Corps by the Military Tribunals.

Through 1915, members of the Corps paraded an incredible 259 times. Not all of the same men were able to parade on every single occasion, but they tried their best. The residents of Folkestone became accustomed to seeing men in uniform in their midst, and it must have given them a certain feeling of security.

In November 1916 the Corps had 359 members and by September 1917 it had dropped to 254. They joined together with the Kent Volunteer Fencibles to form 'E' Company of the 1st Cinque Ports Battalion. Fortunately there remained an appetite by men who couldn't for different reasons go off to war still to do their bit back home.

With the coming of the end of the war, there was no longer a need for the Volunteers and they were not used after December 1918, although they were not officially disbanded until January 1920 and the motor vehicle section was retained until April 1921.

A letter appeared in the *Folkestone, Hythe, Sandgate and Cheriton Herald* on Saturday, 14 November 1914. It was written by a son, Lance Corporal Samuel G.A. Jones of the 2nd Battalion Grenadier Guards serving on the Western Front in France, to his father, Mr Daniel P.W. Jones of 78 Dover Street in Folkestone, who had then passed it on to the newspaper for them to share it with their readers:

Dear Dad,

This is the first opportunity I have had of writing for some days. This has been a very hard week.

On November 1st we occupied some trenches about 800 yards from the German firing line. As soon as dawn commenced to show the Germans opened a terribly heavy fire on us with their heavy siege guns. One shell burst in our trench just to my left. One man was blown to bits, three men and one officer were buried and several of us were half buried. I soon got free and then went to the help of my chums who were buried. We were so unnerved and excited that I started scratching the dirt away with my fingers. I soon calmed down and managed to find a trenching tool, and dug two out, while someone else unearthed the rest.

None were hurt, only unnerved. We were literally blown out of the trench, and had to dig another. We had to shift out of five lots of trenches that day, but we still held on to our position, and were reinforced by the French. While the shells were falling it was like hell on earth, and it was the worst experience I have ever had out here.

The following day our battalion were ordered to advance through a wood with fixed bayonets, and clear it of German sharp shooters. We got halfway through when the Germans opened a murderous fire on us, from a small ridge in front. We however advanced and occupied the position.

We have not had any sleep for eight days, and no wash for a week. Yesterday I managed a splash in a drop of water in a ditch. Notwithstanding, we are all merry and bright and quite confident of success ultimately. We have just heard a rumour of a large naval victory of our fellows, but it has not been confirmed. We have plenty of tobacco and cigarettes, thanks to the 'Weekly Dispatch' and other papers. Last night we were heavily attacked, but held them off all right.

We are all in great hopes that the War will be over by Christmas. I am speculating on how many times Kaiser Bill will be burnt on the 5th in England.

The engagements we have been in up to now are Mons, Landerecies, Villers-Cotterets, Nestles, Baitron, Soupier, Chavonne, Ypres and Reutel.

Samuel G.A. Jones, now Sergeant (13278), sadly died just six weeks later, on 3 January 1915. He was wounded during fighting near Bethune, and subsequently died of his wounds. Samuel had two elder brothers, Lewis and Daniel, but I was unable to establish whether either man served during the war.

Another really interesting letter, written by Bandsman F. Finchman of the Royal Irish Fusiliers, was received by the *Folkestone, Hythe, Sandgate and Cheriton Herald* and appeared in the edition of Saturday, 21 November 1914. Some of his initial training, before going out to

France, had been at Shorncliffe Barracks. He had fond memories of his time spent in Folkestone and felt compelled to write about his experiences and send his words to the local newspaper:

I thought I would drop you a line to let you know I have not forgotten my old acquaintances at Shorncliffe. I am pleased to say all the football team are well, and last Sunday my company were relieved for 48 hours from the trenches to get a shave and a wash, the first for ten days, and in the afternoon we played a football match between the headquarters staff and my company. The players included the following, with whom you are well acquainted: Captain Kentish, Captain Hill, Lieutenant Barefoot, Sergeant Seagrott, Corporal Atkins, Privates Griffin, Doyle, Cummins and myself. The referee was Sergeant Stoner of the RAMC, who is in charge of our medical detachment. We only played twenty minutes each way as lying in a narrow trench is not conducive to good training is it?

The Commonwealth War Graves website records a Captain Harold Edward Kentish of the 281st Army Troops Company, Royal Engineers, who was killed in action on 30 March 1918. His name is commemorated on the Pozières Memorial which is situated in the Somme region of France.

There were a total of twenty-five Captain Hills killed in the First World War, but none from the Royal Irish Fusiliers. Lieutenant Barefoot survived. Sergeant (6663) Albert E. Seagrott, of the 1st Battalion, Royal Irish Fusiliers, was killed on 24 May 1915. He has no known grave and his name is commemorated on the Ypres (Menin Gate) Memorial. Sergeant Stoner appears to have survived and made it through the war, as did Corporal Atkins and Bandsman Finchman. There were two Private Griffins of the Royal Irish Fusiliers who died in the First World War, it could have been either one of them, or possibly neither. The regiment had eight Private Doyles who died, and Private (11377) Daniel Cummins of the 2nd Battalion, Royal Irish Fusiliers, was killed on 15 March 1915. His name is commemorated on the Ypres (Menin gate) Memorial.

It is somewhat strange reading the first part of that letter, only to then discover that as many as five of the men he mentioned were quite possibly dead by the end of the war.

His letter continued,

The Germans were shelling a village about half a mile away, but not near enough to interfere with our game, though you would have laughed when a German aeroplane came over our heads, and we all had to lie flat on the ground until it passed over us. I really did enjoy the game, which resulted in a win for the staff by three goals to one.

Well, we left for the trenches the same night as soon as it got dusk, and the Germans must have seen some of the troops moving, as we had hardly got into the trenches when they opened fire with maxim guns and rifles. They were, however, just a bit too late, as we were under cover and returned their compliments with interest. We are only about 500 yards away from their trenches, and both sides are continually firing at one another. As soon as anybody shows himself, bang a bullet at him.

You, of course know how chummy our fellows and the Seaforths were when we were at Shorncliffe. Well, it is just the same out here. We have been working together all the time, and it was a great sight when both regiments charged the German trenches here. About a week ago we crept up to within 30 yards of them and ran at them. The roars of them were terrible and we took 63 prisoners that day and killed a lot. Both regiments honoured the dead together in a little cemetery we made near the village. Unfortunately it has been added to now, and there must be 50 or more buried there.

Well sir, I expect football is pretty slack round Folkestone. By all accounts Folkestone has had to bear the brunt of the Belgian refugee invasion, and from what I have read in the newspapers, there have been some pathetic sights over at Folkestone, though goodness knows I have seen things out here that would make anyone's heart bleed. When the Germans get into a town or village they seem to destroy everything they can lay their hands on, just for the sake of destruction, as they cannot take half the things away with them. If they could, they would not be of any use to them.

They tried a new shell on the jocks the other day. I should imagine it was fired from a sort of field mortar as it throws a projectile about three feet long, and you can see it coming through the air. It struck a house which some of the Seaforths were holding, and the place collapsed like a pack of cards, killing, I believe, twenty men and wounding a lot more…

I expect you have heard of the death of Captain Carberry. He was shot from a cellar of a farmhouse, which about a dozen of the Germans had run into. They killed six of our chaps, and we could not get them at all, as when anyone entered the gateway, he was shot at once. So at night time the engineers came up with gun cotton, and blew the place up. Only one of them came out alive, and he laughed when he saw the dead bodies of our chaps, but it was the last laugh he ever did on this earth, for the General gave the orders for him to be shot, as they had committed pure murder, and it was not warfare.

It was surprising that a letter which carried that amount of personal detail and information made it through the official censor, especially so soon after the events had taken place. It certainly gave a flavour of just how bloody and brutal the war actually was.

CHAPTER THREE

1915 – Deepening Conflict

At the outbreak of the war the Canadian Army consisted of just 3,000 men. It was, in essence, no more than a part-time militia. Within the first couple of days of the war over 30,000 men had voluntarily enlisted in the Canadian Army, and as the war gathered momentum so the number of those young men wishing to enlist increased rapidly.

Canadian Soldiers at Shorncliffe Camp attending Mass

In February 1915 a force of 40,000 fit, young Canadian soldiers arrived in England at Plymouth. From there they took trains to their new temporary home at Shorncliffe Camp on the outskirts of Folkestone. Like their British counterparts, they too had been told it would all be over by Christmas, once they had given the Germans a 'bloody nose'. To most, this was an adventure not to be missed, a bit of excitement that they could tell their grandchildren about when they were old men, a chance to go to England free of charge and take part in a great experience, a nice change from their normal and laborious lives back home.

Shorncliffe Army Camp had first been established as far back as 1794, but during the First World War it was used as a staging post for mainly British troops who were destined to serve and fight on the battlefields of the Western Front. Nine months after the outbreak of the war it became a training location for the Canadian Army. Between September 1917 and a month after the Armistice had been signed, it was also home to the Canadian Army Medical Corps, who treated their own wounded soldiers in general hospitals that had been based at the camp.

On the morning of Monday, 15 February 1915, it wasn't the war which placed the town of Folkestone in the news, it was the discovery of the headless and naked body of an infant child which was found on the Harbour branch of the railway. Close to where the body was discovered was a smashed medicine bottle and some baby items. With these items to hand, Inspector Lawrence began his enquiries. By the following afternoon (Tuesday) the policeman had made an arrest. The evidence he had gained led him to 19 Palmerston Street where he arrested a married woman by the name of Margaret Hannah O'Neale, who was lodging there. She was using the surname of Williams, but initially informed Inspector Lawrence that her name was Sharp. She then lied to him concerning the whereabouts of her daughter, initially claiming that a Mrs Forman was looking after her child, but she seemed to have forgotten where the woman lived. The next morning, Mrs O'Neale, a middle aged woman, thin and tall in stature and plainly dressed, was placed before the town's magistrates, Mr J. Stainer, Mr G.I. Swoffer, Mr R.J. Linton, Councillor G. Boyd, Alderman F. Hall, Councillor A. Stace, and Mr E.T. Morrison, who charged her with wilfully murdering her eight-month-old daughter, Phyllis Annie O'Neale. The court heard from PC Craddock that he was on duty on Monday morning at the Harbour Pier when, as result of information received, he made his way to the Harbour branch of the railway, between the Junction and the Harbour Railway station, to a point about eighty yards below Radnor Bridge. Near there was a public footpath which connected North Street with East Cliff. He arrived there at 7.45 am and immediately saw the headless body of a naked female child which was lying on its right side. He also noticed a total lack of blood anywhere in the vicinity, indicating that the victim had been killed somewhere else and the body dumped there at a later time. He discovered a broken medicine bottle near to the body. On the bottle were the words, 'Half a teaspoon to be taken three times daily.' The word 'Half' had been written over the word 'one', which had then been crossed out. There were several employees of the South Eastern Railway Company already at the scene when PC Craddock arrived, one of them was Arthur Arnall of 68 Dudley Road, Folkestone. PC Craddock picked up the lifeless body of the young child and removed it to Folkestone Police Station before then taking it to the mortuary. At about 10 am the same morning PC Craddock returned to the location where the child's body had been discovered, with Inspector Lawrence. There they found a baby's dummy (referred to as a comforter), a baby's sock which had been cut in to two pieces, two safety pins, and a piece of broken earthenware which had traces of blood on it.

The next witness was Mrs Elizabeth Margaret Kendall, the wife of John Kendall, a painter. The couple were the owners of 19 Palmerston Street, Folkestone, the address at which Mrs O'Neale was arrested. She confirmed that Mrs O'Neale had been renting a furnished bedroom in her home since about the middle of October 1914, along with a daughter, Phyllis, who she estimated to be about five months old. When she first rented the room she explained that her name was Mrs Williams and that her husband was a soldier in the Berkshire Regiment. She told Mrs Kendall that she would return later that evening with her husband, to finalise the agreement for the room. True to her word, later that evening she returned with a man in Army uniform who she introduced as her husband, Mr Williams. Six shillings was agreed as a weekly rent, and paid in advance by Mrs Williams. They remained there until

Saturday, 13 February, when they were given notice by Mrs Kendall to leave. During the time they had stayed at her property, Mr Williams had not stayed there all the time, on average about twice a week. Mrs Kendall also made mention of noticing that although a pretty child, it appeared somewhat frail and small for the age of five months and she was often crying.

The third witness was Mrs Annie Dorothy Tuff, a widow, who lived at 22 North Street. She said that the accused was her sister, Margaret Hannah, and that she was about 36 years of age. She confirmed that she was married, but to Ernest John O'Neale, whom she had married sometime around 1899. They had three children but had been living apart for the previous nine years. Mrs Tuff confirmed that she knew of her sister's baby daughter and that it had been born sometime in the middle of June. (The 1911 census showed that Margaret Hannah Neale and her three children, Cyril, Ida and John, were all living with Annie Tuff at 22 North Street, Folkestone.)

Bergari Rose, who lived at 64 Tontine Street, Folkestone, and who let out rooms, gave evidence to the fact that he rented a room to a woman on the evening of Sunday, 14 February, for two shillings. She had arrived at his home late in the evening at between 8.30 pm and 9.15 pm. Mr Rose could not be one hundred per cent sure that the accused was the same person, as he believed the woman who booked the room to have been taller. He did remember that the woman did not have a baby with her, only a small parcel that she was carrying under her arm. He later identified the prisoner in a line-out parade at Folkestone Police Station as being the person who booked a room at his home on 14 February.

The Chief Constable, Mr H. Reeve, informed the magistrates that he had taken the matter as far as he could up until that time, and asked that the prisoner be remanded in custody for a further week, so that he could continue with his enquiries as expediently as possible. The prisoner was remanded in custody.

On the morning of Thursday, 18 February, Inspector Lawrence's enquiries took him to 44 High Street, Cheriton, where Mrs O'Neale had apparently stayed on Monday night. The house was owned by a widow, Mrs Adeline Bush. She had rented a furnished bedroom in her home to Mrs O'Neale at about three o'clock in the afternoon on

Monday, 14 February, telling Mrs Bush that she was renting the room for her and her husband. A price of five shillings a week was agreed. At about eight o'clock that same evening Mrs O'Neale returned with a man in uniform who she said was her husband. They had no luggage but Mrs Bush noticed that Mrs O'Neale was carrying a small parcel. The soldier left the house at around 6 am on the Wednesday and Mrs O'Neale left at about 3 pm later the same day. Inspector Lawrence called at the address on the Thursday and Mrs Bush took him up to the room that they had rented, which no one else had rented since. She watched while the Inspector searched the room and saw him remove a parcel from between the mattress and springs of the bed. He untied it and she could see that it contained the head of a child.

Mrs Kendall of 19 Palmerston Street, from whom the prisoner had rented a room, recalled that when she called at her home on the Monday morning the child's body was discovered, she had with her a brown paper parcel and that after she had vacated the room, a partly burnt, blood-stained piece of newspaper was discovered in the fire grate of the room.

Inspector Lawrence then produced the gruesome piece of evidence that was in fact the head of an infant female child. On seeing the head, Mrs O'Neale became visibly ashen, showed signs of emotion and appeared to be about to faint. A glass of water was provided for her. Prior to this Mrs O'Neale had appeared to be totally unconcerned about the proceedings and their implications, especially for her. Mrs Kendall identified the head as that of baby Phyllis O'Neale, the daughter of the accused.

The soldier who had been referred to by the name of Williams was called next. The coroner asked him if he and the prisoner were husband and wife. He replied that they were not. The coroner asked him if he wished to give evidence and Williams stated that he did. He informed the inquest that his name was John Williams and that he was a private in the 5th Battalion Royal Berkshire Regiment, and was stationed at St Martin's Plain, Shorncliffe. He said that he knew the woman as Margaret Neale, and that he had known her since the beginning of September the previous year. He had met her one evening at the Clarendon hotel in Folkestone. They had started seeing each other and began living together in about November. He said that at first he did not know that she had a child and only found out sometime later. He explained that for different reasons he hadn't seen much of her over the weekend of 12 and 13 February. The last he had seen of her was about two o'clock on the Saturday afternoon at the Victoria pub, when she had the child with her. The next time he saw her was about 1 pm on Monday afternoon when she turned up at his barracks at Shorncliffe with his washing. He noticed that she had another parcel with her but he did not enquire what it was. She didn't have the child with her and when he enquired where it was she told him, 'they were minding it for her down at North Street.'

On the second day of the inquest, Friday, 19 February 1915, a dramatic and shocking turn of events took place. With all of the witnesses having given their evidence, the coroner asked Mrs Neale if there was anything that she wanted to say. She stood up, moved forward slightly, and with emotion clearly visible in her eyes, she said, 'I did do it. I am sorry. I did do it.' She then broke down and wept uncontrollably. Her sister, Mrs Tuff, on hearing her admission called out 'Oh Hannah!' and also began to cry.

After a short time, Mrs Neale managed to regain her composure. She was advised by the coroner not to say anything further, because although she was not on trial, what she said could be used against her in any future hearings.

She was being led quietly from the court after having been admitted to the next assizes at Maidstone. As she passed Private John Williams, who was seated in the court, she turned to him and said, 'Goodbye'. As she leant over to kiss him, she broke down, once again crying uncontrollably, and then she had to be physically carried from the court.

The next assizes at Maidstone were held on Saturday, 19 June 1915, Justice Darling presiding. Mrs Hannah Neale was defended by Mr Thesiger, who had advised her to plead not guilty and her defence would be that of temporary insanity. Justice Darling wasn't having any of it. The jury found her guilty of the offence of wilful murder, taking just ten minutes to reach a verdict, but they did add a strong recommendation for mercy. Despite this, Justice Darling donned his black cap, confirmed the jury's finding of guilty and passed the death sentence, but told Mrs Neale that he would pass the jury's recommendation on to the proper quarter.

Remembrance Road leading down to the Harbour

I can find no record of Hannah Neale having been hung, so I am going to assume that her death sentence was changed to one of life imprisonment.

Corporal (45770) John Williams, who was with the 5th Battalion, Royal Berkshire, Regiment, died of his wounds on 5 October 1918. He had previously served as a private (18815) in the Oxford and Bucks Light Infantry. He was 22 years of age and is buried at the St Sever Cemetery Extension, Rouen, France.

One of the most popular cafés for British soldiers during the First World War was in Folkestone. It wasn't frequented by the rich and famous, it wasn't located in a posh part of town, and it wasn't renowned for selling a particular type of tea or a signature item of food. Mole Café could be found in Folkestone Harbour, specifically on the platform of the harbour's railway station. It was literally at the very end of the line. This is where British 'Tommys' would have their farewell cup of tea, and their last cake or bun before they crossed over the Channel to go and fight on the Western Front. For many it was sadly a one-way trip, making their visit to Mole Café a once in a lifetime opportunity.

During the First World War it is estimated that as many 10,000,000 passengers left Folkestone Harbour on route to Boulogne. The vast majority of these were soldiers, but there were many nurses among their number. The embarkation of troops leaving Folkestone became such a well-drilled process, that those in charge could have done it with their eyes closed by the end of the war, they had done it so many times.

Most troops wouldn't have been in the town that long prior to leaving, for they would have conducted their basic training at other locations around the country, and would have come to Folkestone only to hitch a ride across the Channel.

Troops would be assembled on Folkestone's sea front promenade, known as the Leas, outside one of the town's finest hotels, the aptly-named Grand, a stopover that would have been popular with many of society's rich and famous. Once the order 'step-short' was given, off they went on their journey to the harbour, which was made easier because of the steep decline of the road, aptly-named Slope Road, although after the war this was changed to the Road of Remembrance and a memorial to those brave young men who had taken the walk was erected at the top of the hilly road in the form of a short obelisk.

Some 43,500 men and women either left their signature or wrote their name in one of the visitors' books which were left on the small wooden table under the flags in the café. As a percentage of the estimated numbers that left Folkestone to go off to war, it is very small. If the estimated number of men and women who left the country via Folkestone Harbour is correct, that would mean that less than half a per cent of them left their names in one of the books. There are reasons for this. The first of the books was signed on 9 June 1915, by which time the war was already more than ten months old. But one of the biggest factors is that literacy back in 1915 was still quite poor. Not everybody could read and write back then.

Three women were the brains behind the café: Mrs Stuart, and sisters Florence and Margaret Jeffrey. Between them they came up with the idea to serve cups of tea and provide cakes and buns, free of charge, to the brave young men and women who were leaving to go off to war. This they managed to achieve with the help of an array of local women volunteers. It was an amazing gesture of human kindness, with absolutely no ulterior motive attached to it. Florence and Margaret would later be made members of the Order of the British Empire (OBE), in recognition of their wartime efforts. I have been unable to find out for sure whether Mrs Stuart was similarly rewarded.

The last of the eight books were signed on 29 October 1919. Besides

Mole Café in Folkestone Harbour

officers and men of His Majesty's Army, there were some very famous political as well as royal dignitaries who visited the humble café and left their monogram in one of the books. One of the most famous was Winston Churchill, who signed it on 16 September 1919, when he held the position of Secretary of State for War.

Rest Camps became a part of Folkestone during the First World War. An eyesore to some, for the soldiers who had cause to use them they were a godsend, and a necessity in the circumstances. Managing the large numbers of soldiers arriving in Folkestone in readiness to board ships was no mean feat. It took meticulous planning to make it work like clockwork and, as always, the best laid plans can go awry. In most cases, delays were caused by problems in the Channel, either extremes of the weather, or the presence of German submarines or mines. The weather conditions could be a real problem, especially in the winter months. When crossings had to be cancelled, thousands of men might be delayed for a day or longer. They needed feeding and a roof over their heads for the night. If the numbers were small, they could be billeted in the homes of Folkestone, but larger numbers could pose a problem. It was recognised early on in the war that this was a real issue and one that needed addressing as expediently as possible. So it was that Colonel Burns-Begg was sent to Folkestone by the War Office in August 1915 to set up a number of Rest Camps in the town. No easy task. For him to be able to effectively carry out his role, he was provided with the newly created position of Town Commandant, Folkestone. His position also made him a powerful individual in other arenas besides the Rest Camps, as the title carried with it the additional duty of being the competent military authority for Kent (although that didn't include the Dover Defence area or the Thames and Medway Defence areas).

Initially on arrival in Folkestone, Colonel and Mrs Burns-Begg stayed at the Burlington Hotel in Earls Avenue. In September 1915, while still staying at the hotel, Mrs Burns-Begg was advertising in the local newspaper for a 'Plain Cook' and a 'Parlour Maid', one would assume in readiness for moving into a nearby property.

In December 1915, Colonel Burns-Begg issued an order under the Defence of the Realm (Consolidation) Regulations 1914 in relation to the sale of alcohol to troops. It stated that as from 18 December 1915 all licensed premises within the municipal boroughs of Folkestone and Hythe, as well as the urban district of Sandgate, would be closed at all hours for the sale or supply of intoxicating liquor to members of His Majesty's forces or to any person acting on their behalf, for consumption off the premises.

Marine Gardens Folkestone

A number of properties were acquired in the area of Marine Parade and Marine Terrace and were hastily turned into the town's first Rest Camp, or No.1 Rest Camp. The camp was fitted with a large cookhouse, sufficient to provide food for the 2,200 men it was possible to accommodate. Because of the large number of soldiers that could be staying at the camp at any one time, it was decided that it needed a commandant to oversee its running. This honour fell to Major H.F. Sparrow, with his assistant commandant being Major G.C. Grahame.

In May 1916 No.2 Rest Camp was opened in Folkestone, which could cater for a maximum of 1,000 men. This time it wasn't in a well-equipped building, with pleasing views looking out to sea, it was in a large field, situated off Bathurst Road. The accommodation at this camp consisted of men having to sleep in large tents with the use of a large stove in the middle of each one to stave off the cold night air, which could be severe in the winter months.

Even though by 1916 there were two Rest Camps in place, the authorities knew that more were going to be needed. In early 1917 No.3 Rest Camp came in to being after a number of properties had been acquired in the area of the Leas by Clifton Crescent. The newly-promoted Lieutenant Colonel H.F. Sparrow was moved over from No.1 Rest Camp to be the commandant with Major E.L. Hunter MC as the assistant commandant. Major G.C. Grahame took over as commandant of No.1 Rest Camp.

No.3 Rest Camp was bigger than the first two camps put together. It could cater for 5,000 officers and men. For some reason the slightly unusual decision was taken to install a dairy at the camp, allowing butter to be made.

It would appear that the use of the word 'acquired' was a euphemism for the word 'commandeered'. A meeting of the General Purposes Committee at Folkestone Town Hall on Tuesday, 14 November 1916, shows that the houses which became No.3 Rest Home had been commandeered under the Defence of the Realm Act, which resulted in the owners and occupiers of the premises having to move out. The Government paid rent to the owners based on the assessable value of the properties. Where needed, applications could be made for an advancement in relation to the rent. Any claims that owners wished to make in relation to any loss of trade, cost of removals or any damage caused to the property had to be brought before the commission for them to decide upon.

Regrettably Colonel Robert Burns-Begg wasn't able to see what he had started fully come to fruition as in October 1917 he had to be replaced due to ill-health. Whilst on sick leave in Scotland, he died of pneumonia on 9 January 1918, and is buried in Kinross Cemetery.

In May 1917 the last of the Rest Camps came into being when the Drill Hall in Folkestone, which was previously home to the 1st Volunteer Battalion, the Buffs and the Cinque Ports Artillery, was turned in to No.4 Rest Camp.

Lieutenant C.A. Allen, of the Royal Fusiliers, but who at the time was attached to the Royal Sussex Regiment, was awarded the Military Cross for his actions on 21 October 1916, and also promoted to

R. Burns-Begg

the rank of Captain. By the end of the war he had been further promoted to the rank of Major. Before the war he had been an assistant master in what was then called the mixed department at Christ Church School in Folkestone. In 1915 he decided that he had to do his bit for his king and country and enlisted as a private in the Norfolk Regiment, although soon afterwards he received his commission.

Only three days after he arrived in France he was shot, but not killed, by a German sniper while observing their lines through a periscope. The sniper's bullet hit the periscope and caused the glass in it to shatter, a piece of which caught Allen in the corner of one of his eyes. Thankfully, he did not receive any major injury as a result of the shooting. The citation for his award of the Military Cross, reads as follows:

For gallantry and good leading displayed at XXXX section on October 21st 1916. Throughout the battle, and on the preceding days, and under the most adverse conditions, this officer's unvarying cheerfulness greatly inspired the men. During the operations he worked with untiring energy, and although his company were much fatigued, the rapidity with which he moved his men to reinforce was brilliant. He repeated his visits to the

HMHS Anglia (Wikipedia)

front line through intense shelling and his excellent reports that were sent back to his commanding officer proved that he had complete control of himself and his men. His great power of command, cheerfulness of manner, and disregard of danger won for him the admiration of all officers, NCOs and men.

The vessel HMHS *Anglia* was first launched as a passenger ferry on 20 December 1899 for the London and North Western Railway Company, plying its trade in the Irish Sea between Holyhead and Dublin.

With the outbreak of the war, and after a refit in May 1915, she became a hospital ship, transporting wounded troops back from Boulogne, on route to Folkestone and hospitals in London and the southern counties of England, to have their wounds tended. HMHS *Anglia* would have looked truly resplendent, painted entirely white from stem to stern, its hull encircled with a green band and large red crosses emblazoned on either side, telling the world that her sole purpose was the carriage of wounded soldiers.

UC-5 *German U-Boat* **(Wikipedia)**

On 6 November 1915 the German submarine *UC-5* dropped four of its deadly mines close to buoy number eight in the Dover Straits, after having successfully avoided the British defensive mechanisms specially intended to prevent such things from taking place.

The *Anglia* had been operating as a Hospital Ship since 6 May 1915, making the two-hour journey from Boulogne on a daily basis. On 17 November she left Boulogne just after 10.30 am. Two hours later, at 12.34 pm, one mile east of Folkestone, she struck one of the mines which had been dropped by *UC-5* eleven days earlier. The mine struck the *Anglia* under her bridge on the port side of the vessel, causing damage that prevented her crew from switching off her engines. Because of the angle at which she started to list, one of her propellers appeared out of the water still spinning, and she began to turn almost in a circle. Trying to get able-bodied passengers and crew off a sinking ship quickly and calmly would be difficult enough, but when a large number of them are bedridden and reliant on others for their mobility, that process would necessarily become a great deal more difficult. The patients who could walk made their way up to the deck, while the others waited to be rescued by the soldiers of the Royal Medical Corps and the nursing staff of the Queen Alexandra's Imperial Nursing Service.

From striking the mine to sinking beneath the waves took just thirty-six minutes, with the ship moving gradually all of the time, not a lot of time to get all of the crew, the 25 medical staff, and the 386 wounded patients, safely off the boat.

Nine men from the Royal Army Medical Corps perished, along with one member of the Queen Alexandra's Imperial Nursing Service. They were:

> Corporal 4998 Harry Daltrey.
> Private 8880 Stanley Billot.
> Private 57953 Edward Clement Doran.
> Private 7647 Frank Albert Hardy.
> Private 11218 Thomas Heaton.
> Private 18703 Ernest Victor Gardner Hodgkins.
> Private 4996 Edward George Victor Mortimer.
> Private 6395 Hubert William Rumble.
> Private 1738 Walter Ernest Worster.
> Staff Nurse Mary Rodwell.

Their bodies were never recovered, but their names are commemorated on the Hollybrook Memorial at Southampton, so that their memories might live on forever.

Twenty-four members of the crew were also killed in the explosion and subsequent sinking of the *Anglia*, and as all of them were members of the Mercantile Marine their names are commemorated on Tower Hill Memorial in London which was erected to the memory of men and women of the Merchant Navy and Fishing Fleets who lost their lives in both world wars and who have no known grave. They were:

> Fireman R Evans.
> Cook J Hughes.
> Lewis David Hughes.
> Fireman John S Jones.
> Fireman Owen Jones.
> Fireman Owen Jones.
> Cabin Boy Albert Frederick Ashton.
> Seaman William Edward Bassett.
> Steward William Henry Callaway.
> Purser N J Campbell.
> Fireman James Redmond.
> Fireman R Stuart.
> Stoker Thomas Owen.
> Deck Boy Thomas Richard.
> Steward Alfred Wallace.
> Chief Engineer George Edward Williams.
> Third Engineer Joseph Williams.
> Second Steward Meredith Williams.
> Cabin Boy Robert Williams.
> Galley Boy Thomas H Owen.
> Seaman Thomas Richard Parry.
> Trimmer Robert Pritchard.
> Fireman John Lewis.
> Quartermaster William Lewis.

Nearly all of the crew of the *Anglia* hailed from Holyhead in North Wales, which meant that her loss brought great sadness to a small and tight-knit community, it was like the equivalent of a PALS unit being wiped out on one day in the trenches on the Western Front.

Tower Hill Memorial for Merchant Seaman and Women.
(Commonwealth War Graves Commission)

Fortunately, a number of ships were able to get close to the *Anglia* before she went down, including the SS *Lusitania*, a collier ship, HMS *Ure* and HMS *Hazard*, and they managed to save many lives that would have otherwise been sadly lost that day. During the incident and while trying to pick up survivors from the *Anglia*, the *Lusitania* herself struck a mine and sank, although her crew were saved.

The *Anglia*, the first hospital ship that was sunk during the course of the war, had been the ship that brought King George V back to England after he met with an accident while visiting the troops in France.

During the course of the war a total of twenty-four designated hospital ships from both sides were sunk by either striking mines, being hit by torpedoes, or being sunk by guns. These sinkings resulted in the deaths of at least 1,228 soldiers, crew or medical staff. Sixteen of these ships were intentionally and deliberately sunk by the firing of torpedoes, which were despicable actions, whichever side was responsible. A further five vessels were either sunk or damaged having struck a mine.

CHAPTER FOUR

1916 – The Realisation

Shorncliffe Barracks played a prominent role in the life of Folkestone during the course of the First World War. It was a barracks and a training establishment for Canadian soldiers, it was a military hospital for wounded soldiers, and as the war continued it also acquired itself a military cemetery.

On 17 February 1916 Shorncliffe Camp (Moore Barracks) was part of a discussion that took place in a sitting of the House of Commons. The person asking the question was Mr Francis Bennett-Goldney, who at the time was the Independent Unionist Member of Parliament for Canterbury. His question was asked of the Under Secretary of State for War, Mr Harold Tennant.

Mr Bennett-Goldney wanted to know if Mr Tennant was aware of the growing dissatisfaction among both Canadian and British officers and men about the conditions which prevailed at Shorncliffe camp. He spoke of the continued neglect and indifference of the health and comfort of a number of Canadian soldiers who were convalescing from their wounds and sicknesses at the camp. Sadly, the issues which prevailed did so because of 'red tape'. There were some 800 beds at the Moore Barracks Hospital which was located within the Shorncliffe Camp and catered for non-commissioned officers and men, mainly from the Canadian Army. The only recreation and living space for all of these men was a comparatively small building, which had the original purpose of being a drill hall, was no more than fifty feet long by thirty feet wide and about twenty-five feet in height. Its flimsy construction was poor to say the least, made as it was of thin sheets of corrugated iron supported by iron rafters. At no point did the structure have any kind of insulation. The only mechanism for heating the building was two small coal- or wood-burning stoves. What Mr Bennet-Goldney found particularly concerning was that many of the men who had to use this room were convalescing, many striving to recover from such ailments as pneumonia, other lung-related problems and rheumatic fever; not exactly conducive conditions for men to make a speedy recovery.

Mr Bennett-Goldney said that this issue had been raised repeatedly by the medical authorities at Shorncliffe over the past two months, but to no avail. He wanted an answer from the Under-Secretary of State for War about what action he proposed to take. Furthermore, he was at a loss to understand why, even though the general officer commanding Shorncliffe had sanctioned the purchase by the Canadians of extra stoves and flue-pipes, once purchased they had then sat idly gathering dust because the Imperial Engineer at Shorncliffe had been forbidden to fit the stoves as had the Canadian engineers as well. The issue appeared to be that the Canadians, frustrated by their situation, had purchased the stoves and flues locally rather than going through the correct channels, which in this case was the engineering officer in control at Dover. His issue, other than his pigheadedness, appeared to be that he had concerns that the Canadians would have to drill holes in the roof of the structure to fix the necessary pipes. Although this was correct, would it not have to be done no matter who carried out the work?

Mr Bennet-Goldney was at a loss to understand why the real problem, the welfare of the Canadian soldiers, appeared to be less of a priority than concerns about holes being drilled in a sheet of corrugated iron. Because of this the men were not only having to endure the continuing cold, damp and uninviting atmosphere of their recreation room, but having to deal with an unbeatable barrier of red tape which was proving harder to defeat than a German-held trench.

The only thing which prevents Mr Tennant's response from being laughable is that it is in fact a serious answer. The reply in full:

The Moor Barracks at Shorncliffe have been temporarily converted into a hospital mainly to deal with minor cases of illness amongst Canadian and British troops quartered at Shorncliffe and the neighbourhood. There are in addition a fully equipped military hospital of 250 beds and a newly built hospital of 200 beds, both of which can be used for more serious cases. Recreation and living rooms are not provided in any hospital, but dining rooms are allowed for about half the number of beds. No dining room existed at Moore Barracks and the Drill Hall referred to was allotted for this purpose, with the approval of the local medical officers, both Canadian and British. Two stoves were first installed, and as these were found to be inadequate, three more have since been added by the War Department, making five in all. The building designed as a drill hall, necessarily lacks some of the comfort of an ordinary dining room. No reports have been received at the Headquarters, Eastern Command, from the General at Shorncliffe or the medical officers concerned that the heating now provided was inadequate. I am asking for a special report on the accommodation of which complaint is made.

How long the compilation and submission of that report took is not known, but this undoubtedly meant many more weeks of red tape before the issues were looked at and addressed, which does not appear to be the correct way to treat brave young men who had fought for their country in a bloody and unforgiving war.

Mr Bennett-Goldney was quite a character. He had been the Mayor of Canterbury between 1906 and 1911 and was also the MP for Canterbury from December 1910 through to 1918. In early 1918 he gained a commission and became a major in the Royal Army Service Corps. He was sent to France where he became an Assistant Military Attaché at the British Embassy in Paris. He died on 27 July 1918 as a result of injuries which he sustained in a motor vehicle accident. He passed away in an American military hospital in Brest and is buried at the St-Germain-en-Laye cemetery near Paris. In his will he left the princely sum of £23,363 2s 1d, which was shared between Sir John Ramskill Twisden, a baronet, and George Henry Stoner, who was a dealer in Fine Arts.

By the end of the year the military hospital at Shorncliffe was still in the news, in the form of a letter which appeared in the *Folkestone,*

Hythe, Sangate, and Cheriton Herald of 18 November. It had been written by Mrs Margaret M Sherbrooke:

Sir,

I am writing to ask if your readers will help us with Christmas gifts for Christmas trees for hospitals, in the shape of little useful presents for the patients, mittens, scarves, comfort bags, clocks, pocketbooks, knives, house wifes, pipes, walking sticks, cigarettes, crackers, pocket pincushions, folding scissors; also would every lady now preparing her mincemeat remember the boys and give some mince pies for our Christmas trees? If everyone in Folkestone would give six each, we should have enough. Christmas cards are also very welcome. Last Christmas in two hospitals every boy found a Christmas card on his pillow with a kindly greeting.

In Shorncliffe Hospital there are 370 patients, and half are Imperials. We should be glad of visitors for Shorncliffe and Moore Barracks, where there is an even larger number. Christmas papers, too, would be appreciated, to be sent to Mrs Sherbrooke. Leas Hotel, President, Soldiers Comforts Club. Thanking all kind donors in anticipation.

(Mrs) Margaret M Sherbrooke.

I must admit to being somewhat confused when one of the suggestions under the heading of 'little useful presents for the patients' was a request for house wifes! [In a service context, house wifes (sometimes called 'hussifs') were a collection of small items such as scissors, needles, threads, etc, to enable men to repair clothing. This was usually contained in a roll-up pouch.] Maybe those two words had a totally different meaning back in 1916. In addition to my confusion on the point is the added mental picture I now have in my head of the requested house wifes then being attached to the Christmas tree.

William Richard Cotter was born in Folkestone in March 1893, the eldest of six sons to Richard and Amy Cotter. He enlisted in the Army on 11 October 1901 at Canterbury at the age of 19 years and 7 months and became a private (6707) in the 3rd Battalion, the Buffs, signing on for twelve years' service, seven years with the colours and five on reserve. Having served his contracted twelve years, he was discharged on 13 March 1914 and was shown to be of good character. He re-enlisted with the 1st Battalion, the Buffs on 1 April 1914 at Hounslow and went on to serve in France as part of the British Expeditionary Force on two occasions. The first time was between 7 September 1914 and 29 May 1915 and again between 20 October 1915 and 14 March 1916. He was a corporal (6707) in the 6th Battalion, East Kent, the Buffs, when he was involved in fighting at Hohenzollern Redoubt in France on 6 March 1916. He died of his wounds eight days later on 14 March 1916 at the Lillers Field Hospital and is buried at the Lillers Communal Cemetery in the Pas-de-Calais. An extract from the *London Gazette* dated 28 March 1916 records these words to describe Cotter's feat of bravery that won him a posthumous Victoria Cross:

For most conspicuous bravery and devotion to duty. When his right leg was blown off at the knee and he had been wounded in both arms, he made his way unaided for fifty yards to a crater, steadied the men who were holding it, controlling their fire, issued orders, and altered the dispositions of his men to meet a fresh counter-attack by the enemy. For two hours he held his position, and only allowed his wounds to be roughly dressed when the attack had quietened down. He could not be moved back for fourteen hours, and during all this time had a cheery word for all who passed him. There is no doubt his magnificent courage helped greatly to save a critical situation.

I have taken the contents of a letter concerning William's death from an entry on the Sussex History Forum, dated 24 February 2015. It was sent by a priest from the Field Hospital in Lillers where he died:

Dear Mrs Cotter,

Your son William, I regret to say, has just collapsed after a serious operation for amputation. He seemed strong and in such good spirits when he came in that I felt assured and full of hopes of his recovery. However, almighty God has disposed otherwise. He will be missed from the Army, he was a great favourite, and so full of bravery. The General came to tell him he was going to be recommended for the Victoria Cross. This no doubt will console you somewhat, but I am sure you will be more pleased to know that he received Holy Communion, and shortly before he expired, the last blessing. His last words were, 'Good-bye, God bless you all.' RIP. I am now going to lay him to rest.

William Richard Cotter VC.

There is a photograph showing William Richard Cotter in his ceremonial tunic wearing his Victoria Cross. As the award was posthumous, this obviously cannot be correct as he had already died before the award had been made.

What is even more remarkable about William's story is that it should never have taken place, as William shouldn't have even been in the Army at that time, let alone fighting in France, as he had a glass eye, the result of an incident when he was a young soldier. There is, however, no mention of this disability on his Army Service Medical record, specifically when he re-enlisted in April 1914, a type of injury that would be sufficient, one would assume, to prevent a man from becoming a soldier.

The following letter is included in William Cotter's Army Service Record:

From the Senior Medical Officer, Western Heights Military Hospital, Dover.

To, The Officer Commanding 1st Battalion, the Buffs.
Dover 29th October 1905

Sir,

I have the honour to report for your information that No.6707 Pte. Cotter, 1st Battalion, the Buffs, was brought to hospital last night by the Military and Civil Police, with a serious wound of the left eye, believed to have been caused by a glass thrown at him by a civilian in a Public House in Dover.
The sight of the injured eye in all probability will be lost.

I have the honour to be
Sir
Your obedient servant
C Stone

Major RAMC for Senior Medical Officer.

A Military Court of Inquiry into the incident took place in Dover on 6 November 1905. The findings of the inquiry as given by the Lieutenant Colonel of the 1st Buffs were as follows:

Opinion

I am of the opinion that No.6707 Private Cotter, 1st Battalion, the Buffs received an injury to his left eye on the 28th October 1905 from some person at present unknown, during a disturbance in a Public House and that the injury will in all probability affect his efficiency as a soldier.

Private Cotter was not on duty at the time and was not to blame for the injury.

C Vyvyan
Lieutenant-Colonel Commanding Officer 1st Battalion,
The Buffs.

Despite the above opinion, William Cotter was allowed to remain in the Army with the 1st Battalion, the Buffs. Five months after the loss of sight of one of his eyes he was disciplined for being drunk in town. His punishment was to be confined to barracks for five days.

William had two tattoos, one on the back of his left hand, a star, and the other, on the back of his right hand, bizarrely, a tomato. What that represented is not known.

William had five brothers, Frederick, Stephen, Thomas, Bernard and Maurice.

Bernard Cotter enlisted in the Army at Canterbury on 7 February 1908 and joined the Rifle Brigade as Private 2664. Bernard was allowed to transfer to the 1st Battalion, the Buffs, as Private 8881 on 12 March 1908 so that he could serve alongside his elder brother William. Bernard first arrived in France on 7 September 1914 and died of wounds received in action six weeks later on 19 October 1914. He is buried at the Comines-Warneton Cemetery in Belgium. Like William he was disciplined on numerous occasions, generally for being drunk, offences for which he was both fined and confined to barracks.

Morris Cotter was born on 28 March 1892. When he was only 16 years of age he became a gunner (430) in the 1st Home Counties Cinque Ports Brigade, Royal Field Artillery, enlisting on 16 July 1908 at Sandgate.   Four and a half years later, on 18 January 1913, Morris decided on a change of scene. He transferred to the Royal Navy and was sent to Chatham dockyard. He survived the war and died in Folkestone in June 1973 aged 81.

Frederick Edward Montrose Cotter was born in Folkestone on 2 June 1884 and died in 1906 aged 22 while serving with the Buffs in South Africa.

Thomas Lawrence Cotter survived the war and died in Canterbury in 1973 aged 85.

Stephen James Cotter was born on 7 August 1886 in Folkestone. He joined the Royal Navy on 3 November 1902 aged 16 as an able seaman (223511). It would appear by researching the Royal Navy's Registers of Seaman's Services (1853-1928) that Stephen deserted himself on 24 August 1906, but while he was a deserter he enlisted in the Royal Field Artillery on 20 September just four weeks later. He was returned to the Royal Navy on 2 November 1906 where he spent time in the cells. On 31 July 1907 he was sentenced to forty-two days, but on 12 August 1907 he was discharged from the Royal Navy as being undesirable for return to the service. Prior to deserting, he already had an undistinguished discipline record, having spent thirty-five days in the cells. He died on 9 February 1914 in South Africa. He was 27 years of age.

On the afternoon of Monday 3 April 1916 the adjourned inquest into the death of an infant male was reconvened at Folkestone Town Hall by the borough's coroner, Mr G.W. Haines.

Emily Willis was staying at the St Gabriel's Nursing Home, Lennard Road in Folkestone, having arrived there, or to be more precise, having been brought there, by a Miss Anslow on 10 February 1916. She had initially presented herself at the Lyminge Workhouse but was turned away because she had other children (even though the workhouse had been wrong to turn her away for that reason).

She had been staying there for about three weeks, generally helping around the house. On Monday, 13 March, she took to her bed, which was on the second floor of the building, at about 9 o'clock in the evening, which, it had been noticed, was her usual time for retiring for the night. The following morning at about 6.45 am she informed Ethel Kate Hodgskins, who worked at the home, that her baby, a son, had been born, but that she thought it might be dead. When asked what time it had been born, Emily Willis stated that the birth had taken place at about 5 am, the best she could make out. She had called out for help but nobody had come. Miss Hodgskins looked at the infant child and also believed it to be dead. She went and called Nurse Waiscott, who also happened to be the person in charge of St Gabriel's. A doctor was called for and, at roughly 9 am, Doctor W.P. Burnett saw Miss Willis's dead, newborn baby boy, after which he officially confirmed the death. Later that day he carried out a post-mortem on the baby's body, and in his opinion the death was caused by suffocation.

Miss Emily Willis, the mother of the dead baby, whose home address was 86 Linden Crescent, Folkestone, decided to take the stand and give evidence to the inquest, despite being advised by the coroner of the potentially serious situation she was already in. She explained that she had woken at about 5 am on Tuesday 14 March and tried to get the attention of the night nurse who, on the day in question, had been a Miss Pike. She called on more than four occasions, but despite her best attempts, nobody came to her room. The baby was estimated to have been born at about 6.45 am.

Miss Willis had previously given birth to four other children even though she was not married, and had previously been described in a medical sense as being simple. Some four years earlier, the coroner had held a similar inquest into the death of one of Miss Willis's other children, who had also died from suffocation. The determination on that occasion was it was an accidental death.

The coroner said in his summing up that there was absolutely no doubt that the baby boy had been suffocated. He also stated that Miss Willis had been down this road with another of her children in August 1909, when a jury decided that the child had accidentally managed to get itself tangled up in its clothes, and that Miss Willis should have been conscious of this when her baby was born. The evidence that day showed there had been gross carelessness on the part of Miss Willis in relation to the death of her baby.

In relation to the latter matter, the jury decided that death was due to suffocation while in bed with its mother, but there was no evidence to show how the suffocation took place. They also stated that they believed the mother, Miss Willis, was deserving of a severe censure. When the coroner addressed Miss Willis, he told her of the jury's views and comments, that they felt she was guilty of a great carelessness, and they wished for her to be censured for her conduct. He pointed out that this was the fifth child which she had given birth to and that if she was going to bring children in to the world, they deserved a proper chance. He told her that he felt that when she had given birth on 14 March, she just looked at the child and covered it up. This time the jury had said it was accidental, but if a similar thing happened to a baby that she might give birth to in the future, then she might well find herself being charged with murder. He told her that he had his own personal views on the matter, but that he would keep them to himself.

What became infamously known as the 'Hythe Canal Murder', which took place on 6 September 1916, finally came to an end on Wednesday 29 November 1916 at the Kent Assizes at Maidstone.

In the dock was Alice Barber, a 36-year-old charwoman from Folkestone. It had been alleged that on 6 September of that year, she murdered her own 18-month-old son George by drowning him in the Royal Military Canal at Hythe. Alice Barber had been married to a soldier but they had been separated for some years. Sometime previously she had become an inmate at the Elham Union Workhouse where, on 14 March 1915, her son George had been born in the infirmary. The pair stayed in the workhouse for some time before being moved on to the Willsborough Workhouse. On 30 August 1916 Barber left the Workhouse with George, and went to pick up another son, who at the time was 9 years of age. Together all three then made their way to Folkestone to go and visit Barber's mother, where they all stayed for a few days. It was difficult for Barber's mother, who wasn't that well off, to suddenly have to feed three more mouths when she could barely provide for herself. On 6 September at about 10 am she left her mother's home with her son George. There was a witness called Coughlin, who also happened to be an engineer who was employed at Elham Workhouse. He saw Barber at about 11 am in the High Street, Hythe, which was about a mile away from the spot where the child's body was subsequently discovered. When she returned to her mother's home at 2 pm that same afternoon, her mother enquired where George was. Barber explained that she had met a Mrs Keeler, who lived in Sandgate, and who had agreed to adopt George, and had then taken him to London. At about the same time as Barber arrived back at her mother's, George's body was being discovered in the Hythe Canal by two soldiers. When examined by a doctor, he was able to ascertain that the body had been in the water for only a few hours and that death was caused by drowning.

Detective Kennard, who arrested Barber, took a signed statement from the defendant, where she repeated the same story that she had told her mother, and when shown the photograph of the dead child, she

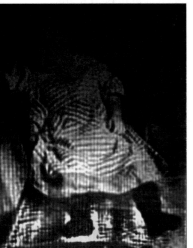

said, 'Oh God, that is my George,' adding, 'Surely that woman has not been and done that?'

When she was formally charged with her son's murder she replied, 'I never did it.'

Detective Kennard informed the court that he had made enquiries at Dover, Sandgate, and Folkestone, in his attempts at trying to find the woman Mrs Keeler, but with no luck.

Mrs Barber gave evidence on oath, starting off with her personal circumstances, how many children she had, and the fact that she had been married to a soldier who had deserted her and their child, and that this had happened about ten years earlier. She said she had lived in Folkestone for a period of time, living with an auntie of hers, before moving

Baby George Barber, looking like he is asleep

on to Dover where she rented a room in a house in Limekiln Street.

Mr Wardley, for the defence, then brilliantly led her through a set of questions about the mysterious Mrs Keeler, what she looked like, where she lived, was she married, how many times had they met, where they had met, what did Mrs Keeler's husband do for a living. Not surprisingly she answered every one of the questions confidently, impeccably and without hesitation, as if she had been through every one of them a hundred times before, schooled in what to say. One of her answers I found particularly interesting:

Mr Wardley: *Did you have any conversation with her (Mrs Keeler) then?*

Mrs Barber: *Yes. She told me she was living down by the Fleur-de-Lys, Sandgate. I had got my little boy George with me. She had not seen him before. She asked me how I was getting on, and I told her I had just come out of the Union [Workhouse] and asked her if she knew of anyone who would mind my baby at so much per week. She said, 'I have taken a great fancy to the child, and I don't mind if I take it myself,' and with that she took the baby.*

It seems somewhat at odds with reality that a baby who the mysterious Mrs Keeler has never even seen before would suddenly evoke the comment that she had taken a great fancy to it and would take the baby herself. Even though 'Mrs Keeler' was never found or located, why would anybody at that time and in those circumstances take on a child that they could possibly ill-afford to feed and clothe, and then kill it almost immediately afterwards? Possibly because there never was a Mrs Keeler in the first place.

Mr Wardley in his summing up concluded that although Mrs Barber's story was a remarkable one, it was the only one she had consistently told throughout the trial. He stressed that he was not suggesting that Mrs Keeler killed or murdered the child, but what he did suggest was that having taken the baby from Mrs Barber and then walked along the canal, she might well have stopped for a moment, placed the baby down on the bank and while taking her eye off it for just a moment, it then somehow managed to roll down the bank and into the canal. On seeing this Mrs Keeler then panicked and simply walked off, leaving the baby to its own devices. If that summing up by Mr Wardley didn't paint such a sad picture, it would frankly be laughable. The jury certainly didn't find any substance to Mr Wardley's words and returned a verdict of guilty, after having deliberated for only a matter of minutes.

Mr Justice Herridge, in passing the death sentence, said that anyone who had listened to the case must have come to the same conclusion: that the verdict of the jury was the correct one. He then had Mrs Barber stand up while he donned the black cap, before officially pronouncing the death sentence upon her.

Clive Griffin was born in Folkestone in 1894 and was educated at

Lieutenant Clive Griffin

The Manor House in Tonbridge. His parents, William and Emily Griffin, lived at 13 Julian Road in Folkestone with their daughter and only other child, Emily. William was the general manager of a local gas company and earned a sufficiently good wage to be able to afford to employ a servant.

At the outbreak of war, Clive gained a commission in the Territorial Field Artillery and in December 1914 volunteered and was put in command of a draft of men who were to be attached to an ammunition column in France.

During the Second Battle of Ypres, he was commended by his division's general for his distinguished conduct in the field. He was later mentioned in despatches and then received the Military Cross for his bravery.

In January 1915 he was sent to Salonika where he was allocated to one of the batteries which was part of the 3rd Home Counties Brigade. He was serving with this same battery when he was wounded. In an effort to save his life one of his legs was amputated, but sadly he died a few days later, on 11 November 1916. He is buried in the Salonika (Lembet Road) Military Cemetery.

His father William Griffin received letters from some of his fellow officers, testifying to his bravery and valour. One of them wrote.

He was so brave and gallant an officer that I shall feel his loss deeply. He was very hardworking, and as he already wears a Military Cross, there is no need to say more than that he deserves it 100 times over. He was wounded while most gallantly commanding his guns in a perfect inferno of shell fire.

A glowing tribute, which one can only imagine would have brought tears to the eyes of his father as he read it. Another said, 'I have a great admiration for his courage, which he has shown on many occasions,' and yet another wrote, 'I consider Clive one of the bravest men I have ever met. He was a lad who knew no fear as he proved when he won his Military Cross at Ypres, and I am sure his commanding officer will never forget him.'

Finer words for a father to hear about what others thought of his son, would be hard to find.

Saturday, 11 November 1916, saw an unusual case brought before the Folkestone Bench, Lieutenant Colonel Fynmore and another magistrate in attendance.

Wilfred Henry Thomas Easton was charged with wearing a military uniform without authority, an allegation to which he willingly and openly pleaded guilty.

Inspector Simpson informed the Bench that the prisoner was brought to the police station by Sir Herbert Raphael, who at the time was an assistant provost marshal for Folkestone, and the person who charged him with wearing uniform without authority. Accused said he bought the uniform in Bow Street, London. He had then somehow managed to get himself on a ship which took him across the English Channel to Boulogne. He said that he tried to enlist but had been rejected owing to being infected with malarial fever. It was also quickly ascertained on his arrival in Boulogne that he was not a properly enlisted and trained soldier and he was sent back to England.

The Chief Constable asked for a week's remand in order that inquiries might be made about the prisoner. He was remanded until the following Friday.

Sir Herbert Raphael, who originally detained the man, appeared happy that this was now a case of a man who had acquired the uniform because he genuinely wanted to join the Army and go and join the fight, rather than somebody who was attempting to gain some kind of advantage by wearing a military uniform. He added that he would endeavour to get the prisoner a light position in the Army. The case was then dismissed.

CHAPTER FIVE

1917 – Seeing it through

Saturday, 31 March, saw a National Service demonstration and Appeal for Patriots take place in Folkestone. The event was in the form of a march which made its way slowly through the streets of the town, stopping at certain prominent locations so that speeches could be given in the hope that some of the town's young and eligible men would sign up and go and do their bit.

It was the end of March on the calendar, the daffodils had begun to bloom, but a spring day it most certainly was not. The bad weather had literally put a dampener on the proceedings. As the procession assembled in Bouverie Square, it was already raining and the roads were exceptionally muddy.

Even with the inclement weather, it was an impressive looking procession. Major H.R.J. Willis, the Commanding Officer of 'E' Company, 1st Cinque Ports Battalion, East Kent Regiment, was at its head. There was a mounted section of Canadian cavalry. There was a military band, members of the Folkestone Volunteers, officers and constables of the Borough Police, special constables, men from the Fire Brigade with their brand new, resplendent, first-aid motor fire engine, Kent 43 VAD, and the Boy Scouts Association.

Sir Stephen Penfold (who was the Mayor of Folkestone from 1913 all the way through until November 1919), along with other councillors and aldermen, travelled the route on board a big yellow bus. The first stop of the procession was at the Baths in Foord Road. It was the mayor who began the speeches by telling the crowd, somewhat depleted as it was, that the reason they were there that afternoon was to ask all men who were aged between 18 and 61 to volunteer for National Service. He drew a comparison between the weather they were experiencing as he spoke to what 'the boys' in the trenches were having to endure while fighting the Germans in similar weather conditions. He said that it was the duty of those at home to do their bit to help the country in the crisis in which it found itself. He noticed that there were women present and he asked them to persuade their husbands, brothers, and sweethearts to do the right thing for their country, and sign up to the scheme.

Others on board the bus followed suit and used hearty rhetoric about the 'way forward' and what people should do for the good of the country. It was explained that the Government simply wanted to know the areas of the country where there were maybe 'too many men', or an overabundance of particular skills, so if need be they could be sent to work in other areas where there was possibly a shortage.

There were cynics who believed that the scheme was nothing more than a backhanded attempt by the Government to ensure that they had a comprehensive list of all the men in the country, so that they could plan their future policy and strategies in relation to the war. In essence, they needed to know exactly how many men they had, so that they knew for how long they could sustain the war effort.

An attractive carrot that had been attached to the scheme was that it guaranteed a minimum wage of 25 shillings. This didn't mean he couldn't earn more than that, it meant that he couldn't earn less.

The speakers used words such as Unscrupulous Monsters in reference to Germany, and The Empire for the side of good.

When the procession reached the Skew Arches, the Mayor and Councillors Martingell and Croucher gave speeches. They certainly were all singing from the same hymn sheet on this issue. Every one of them was pushing the scheme in a robust manner. Mr Croucher had already mourned the loss of a loved one as a result of the war, and his words were some of the strongest: 'It was up to them to volunteer and release another man to go to the front. They could also ask their friends to do the same.'

That really would be a party pooper to come out with while enjoying the company of friends! But Mr Croucher was apparently at home with the idea. He continued: 'Tell them that it was their duty to do so. It was a duty they owed to God and man, and might God bless their efforts.' Mr Croucher seemed bereft of any grasp of reality. Although well intentioned, his words were simply unrealistic if he honestly felt that this was the type of approach that would inspire men to sign up. If anything, it was more likely to ensure that they didn't.

The next speaker, Councillor Marsh, tried a different approach. He explained that Germany's one aim was to overthrow the country and all that it stood for, and that unless more men could be obtained we stood in a very bad position indeed. Then he simply asked the people to volunteer in the name of the king, country and liberty.

The procession then moved on, next stopping at the fish market, where a considerable number of people had gathered. There were more speeches, some of which were good, and some that weren't. The styles of each of the speakers varied. All of them were trying to say the same thing, they just had very different ways of putting it.

The final stop of the procession was by the Harvey Statue, which was erected in 1881 and is situated in Langhorne Gardens near to Folkestone's seafront. William Harvey is often referred to as being 'the father of modern medicine'. He was born in Folkestone in 1578 and died in London in 1657.

The Mayor was the first to speak. He told those present that the purpose of the procession was to gain as many volunteers as possible. He was proud of the effort and sacrifice that the people of Folkestone had made, which was far greater than other towns of a comparable size. Several men had come forward to volunteer that very morning while the procession had made its way through the town, he explained. They wanted men to take the places of those who were doing their part, whether that was by land or by sea, and to uphold the Empire. There was work for everyone to do, and the mayor hoped that the people of Folkestone would do their share in the splendid cause of National Service.

Councillor Mumford used perhaps the best words of the day when he said, 'We are not fighting for gold or territory, but for liberty, peace and happiness the world over.'

The Chinese Labour Corps, as they were officially named, were non-combatant workers employed by the British Government during the First World War whose job it was to perform manual labour thereby freeing up British soldiers for the front line. It wasn't until 14 May 1916, when China declared war on Germany and Austria-Hungary, that Chinese men were allowed to be wartime labourers. Prior to that, the Chinese Government did not allow her nationals to be used in that way.

The Corps was brought into being by the War Office on 31 October 1916 when they sent Thomas Bourne, a former railway engineer who had worked in China for many years, to Weihaiwei, which was at the time a British Colony. China was an impoverished nation in 1914; this was an attractive opportunity to earn a wage.

Although not military in any way, the workers came under the command of British officers, two of whom had served with the 1st Chinese Regiment during the Boxer Rebellion of 1900.

The work that was carried out by the Chinese Labour Corps during the First World War for the British Government should not be underestimated. At the end of the war the Chinese Labour Corps numbered some 95,000 men.

In April 1917, 2,000 men of the Chinese Labour Corps arrived in Folkestone and were put up in a tented camp which had been erected on a large green area close to Cherry Garden Avenue. Then, after a short rest, they set sail across the English Channel to begin their work, thousands of miles from home.

At the end of the war the workers were repatriated back to China. The process began in December 1918. Six of those who had arrived in Folkestone on route to the battlefields of France and Belgium never even made it across the Channel, let alone back home to China. For them, the final resting place was Shorncliffe Military Cemetery:

> Chun Yang Chi
> Chun T'ien Wang
> Huai Niu Yun
> I Lui Ching
> Hsuan Ch'en Te
> Ch'eng Chiao Pi

Albeit as paid labour, they were willing to do their bit for the Allied war effort, and most of them lived and worked in extremely precarious conditions close to the fighting. After the war the British Government gave every member of the Chinese Labour Corps a medal to show their appreciation.

Different size shells dropped by German Gotha Bombers (Wikipedia)

A German Gotha raid took place over London on Friday 25 May 1917, which had devastating consequences for the people of Folkestone.

A squadron of some twenty-three Gotha G.V bomber aircraft took part in a raid on London in an operation the Germans had codenamed Operation Turkenkreuz.

Two of the massive aircraft had to turn back soon after take-off due to mechanical problems, while the others carried on to their intended destination. Though it was a spring day, there was heavy cloud base hanging low over London, which caused the German pilots to abandon their original plans. Instead they diverted to their secondary target which, sadly for the people of the town, was unfortunately the Channel port of Folkestone and the nearby Army camp at Shorncliffe.

By the time the raid was over 95 people were dead and a further 195 had been injured. The dead included 18 soldiers, 16 of whom were Canadians, the other two being British, while the numbers of those wounded included 90 Canadian soldiers.

In the town's Tontine Street, just one bomb was dropped, which landed immediately outside Stokes Brothers, a greengrocers. The street was very busy at the time with workers, women and children either

A Gotha G.V aircraft in flight like the type that attacked Folkestone. **(Wikipedia)**

going about their business or milling about in the street. The death toll was devastating. Sixteen men, twenty-eight women and twenty-seven children were all killed in the subsequent explosion. The following is a list of the civilians killed as a result of the raid:

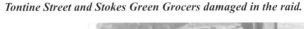

Tontine Street and Stokes Green Grocers damaged in the raid.

Arnold, May Alexandra, was 21 years of age. She was injured in the attack but died later that day at nearby Moore Military Barracks. She was the widow of Bombardier Frederick S. Arnold of the Canadian Field Artillery, 1st Brigade, who had already been killed in action on 25 July 1916, while serving in France. He is buried at the Boulogne Eastern Cemetery, in the Pas-de-Calais. He was 26 years of age.

Banks, Harold Hayward, was initially injured in the blast but died the following day at Westcliffe Military Hospital.

Barker, Mrs Eliza Mary, was 33 years of age and lived at 29 Bradstone Road, Folkestone.

Bartleet, Maggie Grey, was the wife of Sergeant Major Joseph Johnson Bartleet of the Royal Army Medical Corps. He was a career soldier and had been in the Army for many years, having previously served in Egypt, Sierra Leone, South Africa and the Sudan. At the time of Maggie's death, Joseph was 33 years of age. Joseph died on 1 January 1947 aged 63.

Beer, Annie, was 28 years of age and had with her three young children with the same surname all killed in the attack but only one of the children was hers. Her daughter, also named Annie, was only 2 years old. Together with husband and father Ernest Beer who was a marine fireman they lived at 90 Blackbull Road in Folkestone.

Beer, Arthur Stephen, who was 11 years of age, lived at 67 Bridge Street, Folkestone. His father, Henry, was a coal porter.

Beer, William James, was 9. He also lived at 67 Bridge Street, Folkestone, but his father was Harry Beer, a Marine Fireman.

Bloodworth, George Henry, was already a soldier even though he was only 19 years of age. If he hadn't expected to survive the war, the chances are that his thoughts would have taken him to a death somewhere in the trenches of France or Belgium, possibly charging across no man's land as he bore down on an enemy position. I doubt very much he had considered that his death would have come about while he was in the comparative safety of the quaint old streets of Folkestone. George had enlisted in the Army, becoming a private (G/78701) in the 29th Battalion, Middlesex Regiment, before transferring to the 5th Battalion, Labour Corps, where he became Private 149957. He was born in Lee Green in Kent in 1898 and, according to the 1911 census, he lived with his parents George and Mary at 13 Stanton Square, Sydenham, along with his younger sister Ivy and his baby brother John, who was only two months old. George was initially wounded in the blast but died later the same day in Shorncliffe Military Hospital.

Bowbrick, Gertrude Elizabeth, was the 12-year-old sister of Mabel Esther Bowbrick, who was also killed in the attack. Together they lived with their father Walter, who was a builders' foreman, at 31 Ashley Avenue, Cheriton.

Bowbrick, Lily Caroline, was a particularly sad story. She was wounded in the blast and admitted to the Royal Victory Hospital. Her injuries were so severe that she was paralysed from the waist down. She died in the hospital in 1925, having never left it from the day of her admission.

Brockway, Sidney, was 63 years of age and an outdoor employee of the local Corporation. He lived at 17 Peter Street.

Burgin, Dorothy Lilian, was 16 years of age and lived at 21 Old Road, Cheriton. She was a laundry worker. In the 1911 census the family home had been at 7 Railway Cottages, Wembley. Her father Alfred was a plate layer on the railways, while mother Mary had six children to look after. Besides daughters Dorothy and Selina, there were four brothers, Alfred, Charles, William and Frederick.

Dorothy's brother, Alfred Joseph Burgin, enlisted as a private (36349) in the 12th (Service) Battalion, Machine Gun Corps when he was 18 years of age on 15 November 1015, but he wasn't called up until 30 March 1916. He had initially been allocated as a private (17752) to the 4th Battalion, East Surrey Regiment before it was changed to the Machine Gun Corps. He survived the war and was finally demobilized on 28 August 1919.

One of Dorothy's other brothers, George Edward Charles, also served in the war. He enlisted when he was two days from his eighteenth birthday, on 3 November 1916 at Harrow, although he wasn't called up until 22 February 1917. He became part of the 21st Training Reserve, as Private 494893 with the 2nd/13th Battalion, London Regiment. He left England on 23 November 1917 and arrived in Alexandria on 13 December. On 13 August 1918 he was wounded in action when he suffered a gunshot wound to his right forearm. He was treated at the 36th Stationary Hospital in Gaza before rejoining his unit on 4 December 1918. He was a qualified shoeing smith. On 19 July 1919 a board of officers' hearing took place to see if he was still qualified to perform those duties. They found that he was. He was finally demobilized on 22 February 1920 at the Purfleet disposal camp in Essex, where he was placed on the Army Reserve.

Burke, John, of 29 St Winifred's Road, was a boot maker by profession, working out of his premises at Bouverie Road East.

Burvill, Hilda Elizabeth, was 20 years of age and lived at The Cottage, Black Bull Lane, Folkestone. She was the daughter of Albert Burvill, an estate labourer.

Butcher, George Edward, was 44 years of age and a coal carter, of 27 Alexandra Street, Folkestone. He was married to Edith and they lived with George's father Thomas. George survived his injuries for eleven days before he passed away while a patient at the town's Royal Victoria Hospital.

Carson, Annie Elizabeth, was 46 years of age and lived at 24 Military Avenue, Cheriton. She was the wife of Arthur Charles Carson, a barracks warden.

Castle, Albert Edward, was 41 years of age and a naval pensioner and gardener of 27 Wear Bay Crescent.

Chapman, Kathleen, was 16 years of age and lived at Chilham Lees. She worked at the Bates Hotel.

Clark, William, also known as Willie, was only 12 years of age. He lived at Mead Road, and was a boy scout. He was initially injured in the blast but died in hospital.

Considine, Francis Henry, was a 5-year-old boy who lived at 27 Oaks Road. His father was a Canadian soldier.

Cooper, Phylis Amies, was a 10-year-old girl who lived at 3 Warwick Terrace, the daughter of Albert Wallace Cooper, a butcher's assistant.

Daniels, Albert Dennis, was 12, the son of Albert Daniels, a farmer of Coombe Farm, in Hawkinge.

Day, Frederick, was 52 and lived at 4 Linden Crescent. He was a grocer's assistant.

Dicker, Sarah Jane, 41, and Edith Agnes, were the wife and daughter of George Wilkie Dicker, a manager at Maypole Dairy. They lived at 13 Richmond Street.

Down, Alfred Derrett, was 54 years of age, and was the house painter in a hotel by way of work. He lived at 52 Royal Military Avenue with his wife Catherine and their four children, Ada, Rose, Edith, May and son John. There were seventeen men with the name of John Brown who served during the First World War, it is quite possible he was one of them.

Dukes, Florence Elizabeth, was 51 years of age and her daughter, Florence Edith, was 18. They both lived at Horn Street, Cheriton. Elizabeth's husband and Edith's father, Henry Barfert Dukes, was a mercantile clerk.

Eales, Edith May, was 18 and lived at 27 Dudley Road. Her father Arthur was a marine porter.

Feist, Stanley Albert, was only 5 years of age and, along with his mother Nellie, who was also killed, lived at Coombe Farm in Hawkinge.

Francis, Florence, was 33 years of age and lived at 46 Foord Road. She was a dress maker.

Gould, Edward Stephen, was a coal carter in the employ of Anderson and Co of Folkestone.

Graves, Richard Ashby, was a 40-year-old stableman, of Pavilion Stables.

Grimes, Edith Mary, was a typist. She was 24 years of age and lived at 14 Tontine Street, Folkestone.

Hall, William Henry, was 64 years of age and a pork butcher who lived at 68 Tontine Street. William was married to Isabelle and together they lived with their married daughter Charlotte, their son-in-law, Frederick Baker, and their two young children, Frederick and Cecil. William was injured in the initial bombing and died two days later at the town's Victoria Hospital. In his will he left £739 10 shillings, but not to his wife, the monies went to Charles William Beach, a dental mechanic.

Hambley, Johanna Mary, was 67 years of age and the widow of Captain Edgar Hambley, Royal Navy. She lived at 32 Radnor Park Road.

Hambrook, Ethel, was 12 and lived with her mother at 1 Invicta Road.

Harris, Caroline, also known as Carrie, was 33 years of age and lived at 144 High Street, Cheriton. She was the wife of Joseph Harris, also known as Jas, who was a soldier in the Cycle Corps, but had been a potman/barman before the war. Caroline and Joseph had a 3-month-old daughter named Dorothy. There were two other daughters, Florence and Annie. It would appear that they were Caroline's from a previous marriage, as she and Joseph were married in 1909, at which time Florence was already 8 years old and Annie would have been 2.

Harrison, Fanny, was 39 years of age and lived at 15 Bournemouth Road.

Hayes, Martha Godden. Her maiden name was Tumber and she married Arthur E. Hayes in February 1914. Unfortunately there were eleven men with the same name who served and were killed during 1916 in the First World War, and there was no way of establishing with any degree of certainty which one of them it was. Her son Dennis William, who wasn't yet 3 years old, died with her.

Hayward, Louisa Alice, was 37 years of age and lived at 38 Thanet Gardens. Her husband was a serving soldier with the Buffs Regiment. Before the war he had been a tailor. They had married on 4 August 1902 at the Wesleyan Chapel at Grace Hill, Folkestone. They had four children, Winifred who was born on 9 June 1903, Twins Lily and Rose who were born on 19 December 1904, and Amy who was born on 15 August 1910. She had died on the same day as the explosion at Victoria Hospital in Folkestone.

William had enlisted in the Army on 3 December 1915 at Folkestone, but wasn't called up until 30 May 1916, when he became Private G/9986 in the Buffs, East Kent Regiment. He was just a few days shy of his 35th birthday. He first arrived in France on 16 December 1916, with the 6th Battalion, the Buffs. His Army Service Record shows that he was given leave to the United Kingdom between 1 and 10 June 1917; one would imagine this was connected to the death of his wife. On 28 June he was wounded when he received gunshot wounds to one of his knees and his right hand. He was initially treated at a Field Ambulance but was then transferred to No.17 Casualty Clearing Station. From there he was transferred on 15 July to No.7

Canadian General Hospital and then to No.6 on 2 August, both of which were at the British Base at Étaples. Having now recovered from his wounds, he was given leave to the United Kingdom between 21 February and 7 March 1918, but on returning to France, after only three weeks he was wounded again, this time with a shrapnel wound to the left arm. After treatment he returned to his battalion on 11 May. Three months later he was wounded yet again, this time as the result of a German gas attack. He was treated at No.4 Casualty Clearing Station before being sent on to other hospitals at Boulogne and Étaples. He rejoined his (6th) Battalion on 10 September. At the end of the war he was retained in the Army and remained in France, finally leaving there on 7 July 1919. He was demobilized on 12 June 1919 at the Crystal Palace dispersal Unit.

Hickman, Arthur David, was only 5 years old. He lived at 93 Military Avenue, Cheriton. His father, Arthur David Hickman, was a sergeant major (8873) with the Royal Scots Regiment. Three days before the death of his son, Arthur was mentioned in despatches for his bravery, and six weeks after the tragedy on 7 June 1917 he was given a commission and became a 2nd lieutenant. He survived the war and was further promoted to the rank of lieutenant.

Holloway, Mary Philhemennia and Veronica Mary, who were 9 years old and 15 months old respectively, were the daughters of Frederick Sidney Holloway, a merchant's clerk of 13 Burrow Road. He was married to Alice and they had another daughter, Margaret.

Horne, Edward, was 43 years of age and lived at 8 Radnor Cliff, Sandgate, where he was a butler.

Houdart, Constant. He was a serving soldier in the Belgian Army but had an address of 99 Linden Crescent, Folkestone.

Hughes, Rose, lived at 46 Foord Road, Folkestone. She was 34 years of age and a teacher.

Jackman, Dorothy Bertha, was a 14-year-old school girl and lived at 12 Connaught Road. Her father Jas was an electrician.

Jenner, Oron Alfred Company, Quarter Master Sergeant, 3rd Reserve Battalion, Central Ontario Regiment, Canadian Infantry.

Laxton, Katherine Euphemia, was 72 years of age and a widow who lived at 19 East Street.

Lee, William, was actually from New Elham and was only in Folkestone on that fateful day to make plans to take his donkeys to the sands for the season.

Lyth, Daniel Stringer, was 52 and the verger at Hythe Parish Church. His home was Craigside, Castle Road, Hythe.

Marchment, Jane, was 50 years of age and a domestic cook who lived at 21 Manor Road, Folkestone.

Maxted, Elizabeth, was the wife of a butcher's manager. She was 31 years of age and lived at 5 Grove Road.

McDonald, Agnes Curren, was 22 years of age and living at 12 Connaught Road.

McDonald, Albert Edward Charles, was 11 years old and lived at 30 Stuart Road. His father was a seaman.

McGuire, Ernest Henry, was 6 years old and lived at 15 Linden Crescent with his father Harry who was a marine fireman.

Moss, Jane Charlotte May, and her 2-year-old son Walter George, lived at 204 High Street. Her husband, also George, was a serving soldier with a Labour Battalion.

Norris, Florence Louise, and her two children, daughter Florence and son William of 30 Black Bull Road, Folkestone. Her husband, Alfred Norris was a motor mechanic.

Reed, Mabel, was a 12-year-old school girl who lived at 37 Mead Road. Her father Charles was a cab driver.

Robinson, John Walter Francis, was only 6. He lived at 64 St Michaels Street, with his father, also John.

Rumsey, Florence, was 29 years of age and lived in Black Bull Road.

Stokes, William Henry, was 46 years of age and lived at 33a Harvey Street. His occupation was that of 'fruiterer'. His son, William Edmond **Stokes**, who was 14 years old, also died in the tragedy.

Terry, Edith Gwendoline, was 14 years old and lived at 12 Connaught Road. She was still attending school.

Vane, Alfred, was 36 years of age and lived at 8 Bradstone New Road, where he lived with his elder sister. He died on 26 May 1917 at Moore Barracks Hospital at Sandgate. In his will he left the sum of £1,418 1s 8d.

Verschueren, Hypolite, was a Belgian soldier at staff headquarters and lived at 41 Sandgate Road, Folkestone.

Walton, Doris Eileen Spencer, was 16 years old and still at school. Her home was at 25 Bernard Gardens in Wimbledon.

Waugh, Elizabeth Charlotte. Her husband was a serving soldier at the time of her untimely death. Many a wife had been informed of the death of their husbands while they were fighting abroad during the war, but there cannot have been too many occasions when a soldier in the trenches was called to see one of his senior officers only to be informed that his wife had sadly been killed by the Germans back home in Folkestone.

Wilson, Isabelle, was 80 years of age and the oldest of those killed. She was a widow of 11 East Street, Folkestone.

There was much anger among the town's residents about the bombing and the devastating loss and effect it had on everybody. Not surprisingly they wanted answers and explanations. A group got together and came up with a petition that was presented to the Mayor, Aldermen and Councillors of the Borough of Folkestone. It had some 2,377 signatures on it.

> *To the Mayor, Aldermen, and Councillors of the Borough of Folkestone. We the undersigned residents of the Borough of Folkestone, demand that the Government be asked immediately to hold an enquiry into the air raid of Friday last, May 25th.*
>
> *We ask how it was possible for a large number of hostile aircraft to attack the town in broad daylight, inflicting appalling loss of life and damage to property, and if the Military Authorities had knowledge of an impending attack, why no warning was given so that people could return home or take cover.*
>
> *Further, if the statement now public that the Royal Flying Corps were not allowed to go up until it was too late, is true, that the persons responsible should be severely punished.*
>
> *Further, that the Government be urged to take such steps as will prevent attacks of a similar nature and the wholesale murder of the women and children of this town.*

Councillor Forsyth raised a motion that the petition be forwarded on to the Prime Minister, this was seconded by Councillor King-Turner, and the petition was duly carried.

Tontine Street Memorial Plaque.

Such was the furore caused by this attack that questions were asked in the House of Commons, which led to an interesting debate.

Captain Burgoyne, MP for Kensington North, asked the parliamentary representative of the Air Board whether there was any constant air patrol along the east coast, and, if so, whether there was any explanation as to why the recent raid, which took place in full daylight, was not dealt with before reaching Folkestone. He also asked why, although many seaplanes lay ready for instant service in Dover Harbour, no orders were given to their pilots until some twenty minutes after the German aircraft involved in the recent air raid had passed over.

Mr Macnamara, the person to whom the question was addressed, and possibly conscious of potentially giving away too much information concerning British air defensive working practices, answered accordingly, 'If my honourable and gallant friend will place himself in communication with either the fifth Sea Lord or myself, we shall be glad to give him all the detailed information upon the points which he raises.'

Mr Bennett-Goldney, the member for Canterbury, asked a question of the Under Secretary for War, Mr Macpherson. The question was multi-faceted. He wanted to know whether, some fifteen minutes after the German aircraft who had carried out the recent raid on Folkestone had left our shores, an order was given for our own machines to take to the air to give chase to the escaping German aircraft. He further wanted to know whether there were British aircraft that were suitable for defence, in readiness and preparation, waiting to take to the skies. Was it only after such an order had been received by relevant stations that any British aircraft did go up in pursuit? Were the aircraft that were sent up of a type that would have been capable of climbing swiftly to an altitude of 14,000 or 15,000 feet to meet the German machines on terms of equality, and would he now say how many British aircraft actually did take off in pursuit while the German aircraft were near enough to be caught, before reaching the safety of their own lines?

Mr Macpherson's reply could be called somewhat curt in response, but, like Mr Macnamara, he was possibly mindful of not providing too much information which, if explained in detail, might become available to an enemy of the state:'There is no foundation for the allegation in the first part of the question. The answer to the second part of the question is in the affirmative and to the third part in the negative; and the fourth part does not arise. It is not in the public interest to give the information asked for in the last part of the question.'

On Saturday, 27 May, just two days after the tragedy, a special meeting of the Folkestone Town Council took place. The Mayor Sir Stephen Penfold, Aldermen, Councillors and the Chief Constable were all in attendance to discuss the events of 25 May which had seen so much loss, sadness and damage heaped upon the town. The Mayor commented that 'it was one of the most serious things that ever happened to the town, throughout its entire history.' He found the actions of the Germans, 'vile in the extreme,' and added that, 'it was impossible for him to find words to express his abhorrence and indignation of the horrible character of the warfare carried on at the present time.' He also informed the meeting of the numerous letters, telegrams and phone messages of genuine and heartfelt condolences which he had received from numerous different people and from all walks of life.

CHAPTER SIX

1918 – The Final Push

Here are just a very few of the men from Folkestone who did their bit for king and country. Some made it back while others didn't, and there were others who won military awards for their bravery and compassion.

George James Bowe was 21 years of age when he died on 7 September 1918 while serving as a private (G/13628) with the 6th Battalion, the Buffs, East Kent Regiment. He had enlisted on 12 December 1915 at Folkestone and after having completed his basic training he arrived in France on 30 December 1916. He is buried at the Combles Communal Cemetery Extension, which is situated in the Somme region of France. Before the war he had been an apprentice tailor in a drapers shop in Folkestone.

Private George James Bowe

He had a brother, John, who was two years younger than him, and who was too young to have served, only reaching 18 in the final year of the war.

G.A. Kennett was a private (21282) in the 10th Battalion, Canadian Infantry, when he was killed in action on 28 September 1918. He is buried in

Private G.A. Kennett

the Haynecourt British Cemetery, Nord, France. On 27 September the 1st Canadian and 11th Divisions took the village of Haynecourt from the Germans, and the next day they carried on to liberate the nearby village of Sailly. Kennett's family lived at 23 Mead Road in Folkestone.

Robert W.D. Clarke was born in Guernsey in the Channel Islands in 1900, but the family then moved to Folkestone, sometime in the early 1900s. It would appear that the Clarke family had a long military tradition. Robert's father, also Robert, was an Army pensioner. His mother, Marian, was born in India in 1864, suggesting that she was born there while her father was serving in the military. When the family, which consisted of four daughters, who were the eldest, and two sons, moved to Folkestone, they

Private R.W.D. Clarke

settled into family life at 32 Foord Road. Robert didn't enlist until 1918 when he reached his eighteenth birthday, when he became a private (GS/76971) in the Royal Fusiliers. He was wounded while fighting in France in 1918, but he survived the war. He died in Folkestone in June 1948.

George A. Herd was a bombardier (163744) in the Royal Field Artillery when he was gassed while serving on the Western Front in 1918. His family home was at 52 Morehall Avenue.

Private William Richard Cook was born in Sittingbourne in Kent in 1899. He lived with his parents, Richard and Margaret, his elder sister Dora, and his younger brother Herbert, at 49

Bombardier George A. Herd

Chart Road. He was wounded in action near the end of the war but survived his injuries. Herbert was too young to have served in the war, which meant one

Private W.R. Cook

Private Arthur Thomas Archer

less thing for his mother and father to have to worry about.

Arthur Thomas Archer was born in Cheriton, Kent in 1900. The family home was at 3 Victoria Stables, Christ Church Road. Thomas and Minnie Archer had six children, Arthur being one of their five sons. There was also a daughter, named Minnie after her mother. Their eldest son Charley had emigrated to Canada in 1912, and in 1916 was living at the charmingly named Moose Jaw in Saskatchewan. Arthur only enlisted in the Army in the final year of the war due to his age, but that still left enough time for him to be wounded. He was gassed on the Western Front in 1918. His parents moved to 4 Cobbs Mews, Christ Church Road, Folkestone, after the war.

John Charles Beedle was born in 1899. He enlisted on 5 January 1918 at Canterbury and became a private (54644) in the 53rd (Service) Battalion, Middlesex Regiment. On 1 July, John was transferred to the 23rd Battalion, Middlesex Regiment, and eleven days later, on 12 July, he was once again transferred, this time to 'B' Company, 7th Battalion, Royal Fusiliers as Private 78909. On 27 August he was reported missing and later the same day it was confirmed by the German authorities that he had been taken as a prisoner of war.

With the war at an end, he was released from captivity on 3 December and after having being treated at the 4th Canadian Casualty Clearing Station at Valenciennes, as well as the 26th General Hospital at Étaples, he arrived back in the UK four days later and was immediately admitted to the Military Hospital in Lewisham where he spent the next two months. He had complained of having a weakness in his legs as well as sores, or possibly ulcers, on his left leg, which originated from his time spent as a prisoner of war. On being released from hospital he was transferred to his regiment's 5th Battalion. Such transfers were

Private John Charles Beedle

merely paperwork exercises and had no real purpose other than to allocate a man to a relevant battalion that wasn't employed on active service, and normally one that was allocated depot-type duties. Such battalions were full of sick, wounded and soon-to-be-discharged men just waiting for their time to come to leave the Army. He was finally discharged from the Army on 6 December 1919. Before the war John had been a shop assistant in Folkestone, nothing too stressful about that. His parents lived at 2 Sidney Street.

Ernest William Herd lived at 52 Morehall, Folkestone, which was the home of Alfred and Helen Herd and their five children. Ernest was the third eldest of their children and prior to the war his occupation was chauffer.

Private Ernest William Herd

Ernest enlisted on 1 September 1914 at Hampstead and became a private (3392) in the 7th (Service) Battalion, the Rifle Brigade, when he was nearly 25 years of age. Within six weeks of having enlisted he had already been promoted to the rank of corporal, and five weeks after that, on 17 November 1914, he was promoted to the rank of sergeant. He first arrived in France on 20 May 1915, and within ten weeks had been wounded in action with a gunshot to the chest. He spent the next nine weeks in hospital receiving treatment for his injuries. On 27 October 1915, Ernest transferred to the Motor Transport Company, Army Service Corps, where he became Private M2/132560. On 2 January 1917 he became attached to the 54th Field Ambulance, Royal Army Medical Corps.

On 18 December 1917 Ernest received a reminder, as if it was needed, about just how strict Army discipline could be. He had to forfeit twenty-one days' pay for hesitating to obey an order given to him by a non-commissioned officer. How surreal. He didn't actually refuse to obey the order, he simply took too long to react to it.

He was awarded the Military Medal on 1 May 1918. Unfortunately citations for this award were never recorded in the *London Gazette.*

He was killed in action in the field, on 24 September 1918. He is buried at the Tincourt New British Cemetery in Tincourt Churchyard, in the Somme region of France. The village of Tincourt had been a hub for Casualty Clearing Stations throughout 1917 and 1918.

On 8 October 1918, Ernest's mother Helen wrote a letter to the Army Service Corps records department, which at the time was situated at Woolwich Dockyard:

Sir

Kindly excuse the liberty I am taking in writing to you, but am greatly worried concerning my son, Ernest William Herd M/2 132560.

Having heard from his friend in France that he was killed on September 24th, I also heard from friends in London that he is in hospital with gas. So I should be greatly obliged if you could ask his officers if they have any news concerning him.

Yours obediently
Helen Herd.

How sad for a mother not knowing whether her son was alive or dead. On the one hand, a case of desperation while on the other hand, one of hope. But having that glimmer of hope about whether her son was dead or alive would have helped her through what must have been a very traumatic time, even if it was ultimately to be short-lived. By 14 April 1919, Helen, with her husband now dead, and only her daughter Nellie having not left home, was living at 306 Cheriton Road, Folkestone.

I could find no record for the eldest brother, Edward Frederick Herd, having ever served in any branch of the military during the war. In 1911 he had sadly fallen on hard times and found himself admitted to the Southwark Workhouse for twelve days between 15 April and 27 April 1911, before he was discharged. He was a master electrician and a motor mechanic, living at 53 Dover Road in Folkestone with his wife Florence. He died on 2 December 1919 at the South Eastern and Chatham Railway, near Bargrove Bridge, which is just outside Folkestone, possibly as a result of an accident.

Harold Stanley Herd was born in Folkestone on 25 April 1896. Before the war he had been a postman in Folkestone. Having turned 19 years of age, Harold joined the Royal Navy, on 9 August 1915, becoming an Air Mechanic (F7401) 2nd Class, beginning his military career at

Dover. He was discharged on 31 March 1918. Harold died on 17 February 1950. At the time he was living at 69 Morehall Avenue in Folkestone with his wife, Florence. In his will he left her just over £863.

Although there is an Army Service record for a George Albert Herd, who was born in 1880 in Lambeth, London, and who was a private in the Royal Warwickshire Regiment, I could not find an exact match for the George Albert Herd I was looking for, who was born in 1888 in Minster in Thanet.

Frank Edward Young was born on 2 October 1895 in Cherat, North West Province, which was then in India but is now part of Pakistan. He wasn't from Folkestone, in fact there is a memorial cross in memory of him in the Garden of Remembrance in St Mary's Church, Hitchin in Hertfordshire. But during the First World War, his father, Captain Frank Young, was the Deputy Town Commandant of Folkestone, and the entry for his death which is recorded on the Commonwealth War Graves website shows his parents, Frank and Sarah Ellen Young, living at 46 Wood Avenue, Folkestone, so I felt that including his story was relevant to this book.

Second Lieutenant Frank Edwa⟨…⟩ Young, VC.

Frank Edward Young was a second lieutenant in the 1st Battalion, Hertfordshire Regiment, when he was killed in action on 18 September 1918 near Havrincourt, France, during heavy fighting. German forces had counter-attacked against the position Young and his men were holding. His calm leadership must have inspired his men during some four hours of intense battle, which saw him rescue two of his men who had been captured by the Germans. He also took out one of their machine gun positions single-handedly with bombs. He was last seen by his men involved in hand to hand fighting. The citation for the award of his Victoria Cross, which was recorded in the *London Gazette* dated 13 December 1918, read as follows:

For most conspicuous bravery, determination and exceptional devotion to duty on 18th September 1918, south east of

Havrincourt, when during an enemy counter attack and throughout an extremely intense enemy barrage he visited all posts, warned the garrisons and encouraged the men. In the early stages of the attack he rescued two of his men who had been captured and bombed and silenced an enemy machine gun. Although surrounded by the enemy, 2nd Lt. Young fought his way back to the main barricade and drove out a party of the enemy who were assembling there. By his further exertions the battalion was able to maintain a line of great tactical value, the loss of which would have meant serious delay to future operations. Throughout four hours of intense hand to hand fighting, 2nd Lt. Young displayed the utmost valour and devotion to duty, and set an example to which the company gallantly responded. He was last seen fighting hand to hand against a considerable number of the enemy.

Frank Edward Young is buried at the Hermies Hill British Cemetery, which is about eight miles east of Bapaume, in the Pas-de-Calais region of France. He had been commissioned on 26 April 1917, having first arrived in France on 21 January 1915.

His father, also Frank, and a serving captain in the Army during the First World War, applied for his '1915 Star' on 11 February 1919. His home address at the time was recorded as being No.3 Rest Camp, Folkestone.

Archibald Whitehead's mother Esther lived at 33 Rossendale Road in Folkestone. Archibald was a corporal (M2/167147) in the 971st

Motor Transport Company, Army Service Corps, when he died on 28 December 1917. He was 27 years of age. He is buried at the Baghdad (North Gate) War Cemetery. He had enlisted on 21 March 1916 at Grove Park a month short of his twenty-sixth birthday. After completing his basic training, he left via Southampton on 8 July 1917, and arrived in Basra, Mesopotamia, which today has been split into Iraq, Iran and Kuwait, on 30 August 1917. The following Medical Case Sheet forms part of Archibald's Army Service Record:

Corporal Archibald Whitehead
Army Service Corps

Corporal Whitehead was admitted to the 16th Casualty Clearing Station on the 18 December 1917, complaining of pain in the back. He had a temperature of 102 and a prodromal rash of small raised red spots on his thighs, pubic area and on his chest.

On his fifth day of illness, shotty papules appeared on his trunk, face and limbs, the prodromal at this time having almost disappeared.

The following day the papules became profuse on his face and thighs and vesicles began to appear. The rash became confluent on the face, thighs and forearms. Conjunctivitis and ulceration of pharynx and larynx set in.

Patient became very drowsy and his general condition was poor. With pustulation, patient's temperature became hectic and his breathing embarrassed. On the fourteenth day patient became delirious and died.

Treatment, fluid diet, stimulation with brandy. Digitalis given. Morphia, Vaseline and eucalyptus oil used for skin.

Signed
J S Snipe
Captain RAMC

In other words, Archibald died of smallpox. Archibald had three brothers, Ernest, George and Robert, and three sisters, Marie, Alice and Frances.

John Reynolds-Peyton was born in London on 19 January 1896, and while he was still only 12 years old he enlisted in the Royal Navy, on 15 January 1909. By 1911 he was attending the Naval College at Whippingham in Hampshire. He was appointed a midshipman on 15 May 1914. He was further promoted to sub-lieutenant in November 1916, and in January 1918 he was promoted to the rank of lieutenant. He died on 4 November 1918 on board the destroyer *Ambuscade,* of influenza and pneumonia, just seven days before the Armistice was signed.

He was buried at Windsor Cemetery in Berkshire.

Lieutenant John Reynolds-Peyton, RN

His parents James and Alice Reynolds-Peyton lived at 37 Augusta Gardens, Folkestone.

A sitting of the Folkestone Military Tribunal took place on Wednesday, 30 October 1918, in the Mayor's office at the Town Hall. Although not known at the time, the war had less than two weeks to run, and men were still trying to avoid military service.

The first case to be heard by the Mayor and his colleagues was that of George Strood, a local baker. Mr G.W. Haines, on behalf of Strood, by way of mitigation in his client's case brought to the attention of the tribunal the details of a previous case that they had heard at the tribunal, that of a man named Simmonds, also a baker. He had been granted an exemption from Volunteer service on the grounds that he was working each day from 2pm until 10pm and was primarily responsible for the dough. Mr Haines pointed out that Strood had been a sergeant in the Royal Army Medical Corps and was still employed with the St John Ambulance of which he was the quartermaster and secretary, which, when coupled with his work as a baker, meant that he was engaged in most useful work and that, in essence, his client had already been exempted at the same time Simmonds had been. The tribunal agreed.

Another baker, Mr F.H. Sparkes, who was 33 years of age and a married man, applied for an exemption on the grounds of his business as a baker. He did all of the work himself, providing bread for over 200 families, six days a week. If he had to join up he would lose all of his customers and he would be forced to close his business which would affect both he and his wife. The National Service representative commented that the war was far from over, and the government and the military authorities required even more men in an effort to continue the war. He further commented that the tribunal had previously refused exemptions for men much older than Mr Sparkes, and younger men like him were urgently required. His exemption was refused, but he was allowed three months' grace. Luckily for Mr Sparkes, this meant that the war was over when his time came.

A dairy farmer, Mr G.T. Sharp, applied for the rehearing of the case of Mr Childs, who was in charge of the horses on his farm. Mr Sharp told the tribunal that women could not control and look after his horses in the same way that Mr Childs could, which was only to be expected. It was extremely demanding and physical work, which was difficult enough for most men to cope with. As well as the horses, there were 100 cows that required milking every day, and that he, Mr Sharp, simply could not run the farm on his own. Major Willis, the military representative, said that he had been in contact with the Food Controller, who had informed him that milk supply was an essential business, but Mr Childs was a young man and young men were essential to the war effort. Major Willis suggested to Mr Sharp that there must be an older man who could do the work which Mr Childs currently undertook. Mr Sharp replied that he had tried to find such a man but had failed in his efforts. Childs was given a three-month exemption. The National Service Representative, who sat as one of the members on the tribunal, was requested to apply to the Kent Agricultural War Committee for a suitable man to replace Mr Childs at the earliest possible opportunity.

Mr Douglas Spain, who was an undertaker in Folkestone, had applied for a certificate of exemption, stating in support of his application that his was a one-man business, which was run by him in trust for his mother. A large sum of money had been invested in the company and Mr Spain was the only certified embalmer in Folkestone. This having been said, the tribunal was only prepared to grant Mr Spain a three-month exemption. Mr Hall, who had supported Mr Spain in his application, said that he was surprised at the decision as Mr Spain had not been afforded an opportunity to present the full facts of the case before the tribunal. Mr Hall added that in the light of the influenza epidemic by which the country and parts of Europe now found themselves engulfed, there was the real concern that, sadly, many more people would die before it was properly brought under control. The Mayor said he hoped that the influenza epidemic and the war would both be over within three months. The tribunal agreed to reconsider their decision.

Many applicants were given six-month exemptions while a few others received three month exemptions.

Mr G. Brazier, a 26-year-old man from Folkestone, was employed in an Army canteen stores, and was applying for an exemption on the grounds of ill-health. The National Service representative stated that the tribunal had received similar applications at their previous sitting from young men who were employed in Army canteens. Their applications had failed because their work was not of national importance, and it was work that could be undertaken by women. Mr Brazier was advised that he should apply for a protection certificate if his ill-health was preventing him from enlisting; that way he would not have to sit before further tribunals. What Mr Brazier's ill health consisted of, was not explained.

The Folkestone, Hythe, Sandgate and Cheriton Herald of 9 November 1918 carried an interesting article about a soldier who had been awarded the Distinguished Conduct Medal.

Sergeant (495422) Lawrence George Craft MM, of the 2/2nd (Home Counties) Field Ambulance, Royal Army Medical Corps, was awarded his decoration for his actions between 24 August and 3 September 1918 while serving in France. What made his award especially deserving was the fact that Sergeant Craft's unit had been relieved twenty-four hours earlier, but he chose to remain to help the units that had been sent to relieve him and his colleagues. The citation for the award of his DCM appeared in the *London Gazette* on 16 January 1919:

Acting Lance Sergeant Lawrence George Craft

...While acting as stretcher Sergeants near Maricourt from 24th August to 3rd September 1918, these NCOs, [including Craft] displayed great energy and courage, carrying on their work without any relief. They went forward on the 24th August to Happy Valley, and cleared many wounded under intense shell fire, several men being hit at the time. Again under heavy shell fire, they carried in three seriously wounded men, who could not be got at for twenty-four hours on account of the shelling. They both set a magnificent example.

He had already been awarded the Military Medal for his bravery on 2 June 1917. Lawrence survived the war and lived to the ripe old age of 87 years, passing away in 1983 in Thanet.

Lawrence's parents, Frederick and Emma, lived at 43 Warren Road in Folkestone where, including Lawrence, they brought up six children, four sons and two daughters: Frederick, Harry and Leonard, along with

Ada, who was the eldest, and Ethel. All three of Lawrence's brothers served during the war. Frederick and Leonard survived while Harry was killed.

Starting with Harry: Before the war he had been an assistant in a boot-maker's shop. **Harry Alfred Craft** was a lance Corporal (4612) in the 2nd (City of London) Battalion (Royal Fusiliers) London Regiment when he was killed in action on 1 July 1916 on the first day of the Battle of the Somme. Unfortunately, regimental war diaries very rarely refer to men by their actual names when it comes to casualties. The only ones who were afforded that respect were officers, but what we do know is that in the early hours of 1 July 1916, Private Harry Craft, was, along with his colleagues, in the forward trenches at Hébuterne waiting to go over the top. The tension among the British soldiers, after a week of an Allied artillery bombardment on German defensive positions, must have been extreme. Harry Craft is buried at the Gommecourt No.2 British Cemetery at Hébuterne in the Pas-de-Calais, France.

Frederick Thomas Craft was married on 13 July 1916 in the parish church in Hythe to Minnie Ditton. Frederick was already in the Army by then, having enlisted on 11 February 1916 at Ashford, becoming a private in the 4th Battalion, the Buffs, East Kent Regiment. Sometime later he transferred to the 577th Company of the (HS) Employment Company of the Labour Corps, where he became private 315911 and was discharged from the Army on 29 September 1917 for no longer being physically fit for war service. Immediately prior to his discharge he had sat before an Army Medical Board, which had been convened at Thetford Military Hospital. As all of Frederick's Army service had been while he had been in England, his disability wasn't down to having been wounded in action, it was down to an illness or disease which he had either picked up while undergoing his basic training, or that he had already had, which had then been aggravated by his military training. Frederick and Minnie had one child, a son, Ronald Frederick, born on 2 March 1919 at 29 Dymchurch Road in Hythe, to where they had moved during the war. Prior to the war Frederick had been a barman in a local public house.

Leonard Frank Craft, the youngest of the brothers, enlisted on 15 May 1916 at Folkestone, just two and a half months past his eighteenth birthday, although he wasn't mobilized for another ten months, on 23 March 1917. Prior to enlisting, he had been a ticket collector on the railways. He initially became a sapper (347517) in the Royal Engineers, Railway Operating Division. He then transferred to the 4th Battalion, East Surrey Regiment, where he became a private (33578). He later transferred back to the Royal Engineers, where he became a more-than-competent telegraphist. He left from Southampton on 7 February 1918 and, after a journey which took three weeks, he arrived in Alexandria, which is where he remained until the end of the war. His journey home started at Port Said, which he left on 29 January 1919, arriving back in England at Southampton three weeks later. He was demobilized on 18 March 1919 and placed on the Army Reserve. Leonard married Gertrude Agnes Harrington in November 1924 in Ashford, Kent. Gertrude died August 1985 aged 88, while Leonard died in 1991, having lived to the ripe old age of 93.

Another recipient of a gallantry award was Acting Corporal **Horace Walter Williams**, who was born on 6 February 1896 in Folkestone. He lived with his parents, Walter and Mary, at 66 Garden Road. He was the eldest of seven children, which included three brothers, none of whom were old enough for war service, and three sisters. Before the war Horace worked as an apprentice tailor.

It would appear that Horace was part of the Royal Naval Air Service before they amalgamated with the Army's Royal Flying Corps to form the Royal Air Force on 1 April 1918. At the time, the Royal Naval Air Service had a total of 55,066 officers and men among its ranks. The main purpose of the Royal Naval Air Service was reconnaissance. They patrolled the coastline, seeking out German shipping and submarines, and with nearly 3,000 aircraft and 103 airships at their disposal, German vessels always had to be on their guard against a surprise attack.

Horace enlisted in the Royal Navy on 28 July 1915 at Chatham and became an air mechanic (F7013) grade two. During his wartime service he spent most of his time either stationed at Dover or Dunkirk. His last day of service was 31 March 1918, and not only did he survive the war, but he lived a long and healthy life, finally passing away at the age of 94, in Maidstone.

He was awarded the Distinguished Flying Medal, the citation of which appeared in *London Gazette* of 2 November 1918:

> *This observer has taken part in forty-three successful raids, showing at all times devotion to duty and affording the most valuable support to his pilot. In a recent engagement, having shot down an aeroplane out of control, he continued in action, although wounded in the left arm, until his ammunition was exhausted, thereby enabling one of our machines, that was heavily attacked, to regain the lines in safety.*

On the morning of Sunday, 3 November, at the Drill Hall in Folkestone, a ceremony took place, which saw the awarding of Military Medals to two well deserving sergeants.

There was a large turnout of both local dignitaries, which included Councillor Mumford JP and Councillor G. Boyd JP. Men from 'D' (Folkestone) Company, 1st Volunteer Battalion, the Buffs, were in attendance under the watchful eye of Major H.R.J. Willis. There was also a detachment from the Kent No.4 Field Ambulance Section (Folkestone), Royal Army Medical Corps, who were under the command of Lieutenant H.O. Jones. Lieutenant Colonel the Honourable E.J. Mills started the morning's proceedings by carrying out an inspection of the various units that were present. He then presented Military Medals to Sergeant **E.W. Cotterill** of the Royal Field Artillery, who lived at 22 Somerset Road in Folkestone, and Sergeant **Butcher** of the Royal Engineers.

Sergeant Cotterill was awarded his medal for his actions on 9 May 1916, near Ypres:

> *The enemy commenced shelling Corporal Cotterill's battery position. Corporal Cotterill then went round, turning the men out and just as he reached one party, a shell exploded nearby, killing two men and wounding two more. Corporal Cotterill endeavoured to extricate the wounded. He managed to recover one man and place him on the adjacent road, before returning to get the second man, but another German shell exploded, killing the second man and wounding Cotterill. Despite his injuries, Cotterill returned to the first man and with the assistance of some infantry officers, took him to a nearby dressing station.*

Sergeant Butcher won his award for his actions on 9 October 1916 at Guillemont on the Somme. He had discovered that forward communications had broken down. Without concern for his own safety, he at once went forward with a group of his men and successfully managed to re-establish the communications, all the time under heavy German machine gun fire.

The Town Commandant congratulated both men on their fine display of courage and bravery. The ceremony ended with the different units who had been in attendance carrying out a march-past, Sergeants Cotterill and Butcher taking the salute.

Sergeant Ernest Henry Robus

Another man from Folkestone who had been awarded the Military Medal was Sergeant **Ernest Henry Robus** of the Royal Warwickshire Regiment. His parents lived at 12 Greenfield Road. His award was for gallantry in taking charge of his platoon when 'going over the top' and capturing a German position.

The Folkestone Local Advisory Committee covered an area which included along the coast towards Dymchurch, then inland to Ham Street, on to Godmersham, through the Elham Valley and as far as Capel-Le-Ferne. The monthly meeting of the Committee took place on Tuesday, 19 November 1918, at 32 Tontine Street.

The main topic of discussion concerned demobilization and Labour Resettlement. The meeting was chaired by Alderman G. Spurgeon JP and others present included Mr R.G. Wood JP, Mr R. White and Mr Romney, who were the employers' representatives, and Mr B. Noble, Mr R.L. Saunders, Mr W. Williams, Mr W. Collar and Mr B. Bailey, who were the employees' representatives. The Amalgamated Union of Co-operative Employee and Allied Workers informed the meeting that they had been approached by the Ministry of Labour with a view to inviting one of their members to be their representative on the Committee.

It was pointed out that all local labour firms were being sent a form, ED405, which, when completed, had to be sent in to the Local Advisory Committee so that matters concerning employment of demobilized soldiers and sailors, as well as civilian war workers, could be closely monitored to ensure that they were being fairly treated by employers.

Employment had become a massive issue during the war years. Most employers had had no option but to employ large numbers of women during these times, individuals whom they would never have normally employed. The initial apprehension this evoked in employees was only mitigated when they realised they could pay a woman less for doing the exact same job as a man. The real concern of course was that women were not going to be prepared to give up the freedoms which the war had brought for them, and returning military personnel were not only going to be expecting their old jobs back, but to be earning the same amount of money, if not more than they had been doing before the war.

Two days later, on Thursday, 21 November, politics was on the agenda once again, when a meeting was held at Folkestone Town Hall. The meeting was held in support of the Coalition Government and included the Coalition candidate, Major Sir Phillip Sassoon CMG, who received a rousing welcome from a packed audience. Besides the ordinary man, the ordinary woman was present at the meeting, in much larger numbers than would have been normal before the war. The great and the good of local society were also well represented. There were more aldermen than one could shake a stick at, MPs, knights of the realm, justices of the peace, doctors, councillors, and plain old Messrs.

The meeting was chaired by Dr W.J. Tyson who began by addressing those present as his 'fellow townsmen and fellow townswomen', repeating the term 'townswomen' as he undoubtedly understood the newly acquired political ramifications of embracing women in such friendly terms.

The forthcoming general election would be the first one ever in Britain in which women had voted for a parliamentary candidate. The Representation of the People Act 1918 had brought women in Great Britain in to the world of politics for the first time. It allowed for women who were over the age of 30 and all men over the age of 21 to vote in a general election, regardless of social standing.

The 1918 general election was different in other ways. It was the first time it had been held on a single day, Saturday, 14 December, although the actual counting of all the votes did not take place until two weeks later, on Saturday, 28 December. This was so that the votes of British soldiers who were still serving overseas could be transported back home to be included in the vote.

The tone of the meeting was about a way forward to a better tomorrow, while remembering the past and the sacrifices that had been made by so many young men, so that a better tomorrow was actually possible. There was also plenty of political back-slapping for a job well done. The war had begun with the Liberal Party in office, but had been replaced within a year by the Coalition Government, which was made up mainly of Liberals and Conservatives, because of the perceived dithering and lack of purpose of Asquith's Liberal Government. Whereas the Liberals had taken a more 'wait and see approach' and appeared happy to sit back and react to what Germany was doing, the government of Lloyd George had a more proactive approach and a policy of taking the war to the Germans in an effort to gain a decisive all-out victory as quickly as possible. Although the latter approach seemed to have accorded with the views of the general public, it had come at a heavy price, in both a financial sense, and in human life.

Dr Tyson spoke of Prime Minister Lloyd George in glowing terms and drew a comparison with another great British Prime Minister of the past, William Pitt, who in 1783 became the youngest ever British Prime Minister at the tender age of 24. He spoke of his intense love of his country and his great desire to help the underdog in society. He spoke about Lloyd George's achievements and made particular mention of how under his leadership a 'great Education Act' had been passed. He also mentioned the Conscription Act of 1916, as if it were on par with the Education Act. There would have no doubt been some in the audience who might not have been quite so enthusiastic about the Conscription Act as Dr Tyson was. Although it undoubtedly provided the politicians, the military authorities and ultimately the country, with sufficient manpower to gain a decisive victory in the war, it also led to the deaths of tens of thousands of young British men.

Another who spoke at the meeting was Sir Herbert Raphael, the Liberal MP for Derbyshire South. He had held that position in that distant county since 1906, but in truth he was a local man, having lived at Hockley Sole, Capel-le-Ferne, near Folkestone, since 1884 when he had married Rosalie Coster. He was also a military man, having held a commission in the 1st Volunteer Battalion, Essex Regiment, since the beginning of the 1900s. Even though he was a sitting MP at the time, when war broke out in 1914 he enlisted as a private in the 24th (Sportsman's) Battalion, Royal Fusiliers. Remarkably by then he was already 54 years of age. Ten months later, he was granted a commission in the rank of major, and raised the 18th (Service) Battalion (Arts & Crafts), Kings Royal Rifle Corps, at Gidea Park, near Romford. Later in the war he became the Assistant Provost Marshal for Folkestone.

He spoke of new and exciting times ahead and that the time was right for the Coalition Government to go to the country to find out the feeling of the electors on the work that the Government had done and the work which still needed to be done.

The cynics among us might look at that through slightly different eyes. Having just provided millions more people with the right to vote, with the implementation of the Representation of the People Act 1918, the Coalition Government must have felt extremely confident of winning a General Election, especially on the back of having just been victorious in the Great War. If ever there was a better time for a political party to call an election, that was the time. The end of the war and the right to vote was still fresh and prominent in everybody's mind; an almost guarantee for a unanimous political victory. And so it proved.

Sir Herbert certainly knew how to work an audience and say all of the right things that he knew people wanted to hear. He spoke of the Government's support for the hundreds of thousands of returning British soldiers, some of whom would still be suffering from their wounds and some who would now have to deal with their disabilities. They would need homes and employment and the Government would make sure that those who had been maimed would be supported and not simply thrust upon the already over-stretched resources of the country's workhouses. He also spoke of the widows and children of the many men who had given their lives during the war, and promised that they would not suffer; but he did not provide any substance about what his words actually meant in real terms.

Others addressed the meeting, and their themes were similar. This was, after all, a political meeting held for the benefit of politicians, and an opportunity to galvanise the support of the voters so as to secure their own political careers, with promises of what they were going to do for the country and the people in the future. Only time would tell if they ultimately kept their promises.

CHAPTER SEVEN

Folkestone War Memorial

The Folkestone war memorial was unveiled on Saturday, 2 December 1922, by the Earl of Radnor. Originally Vice Admiral Sir Roger Keyes was due to conduct the unveiling, but he had been detained at a conference in Lausanne, Switzerland, where he had been summoned a few days before the ceremony.

Although the weather was fairly good, especially for the time of

The Folkestone War Memorial

year, it was a dull, almost overcast afternoon, with a light mist hanging in the air, perhaps appropriate for such a mournful occasion.

The dedication for the memorial was given by the Vicar of Folkestone, Reverend Cannon P.F. Tindall. The chairman of the committee which had been set up to help raise funds for the memorial, Sir Stephen Penfold, formally handed it over to Alderman E.J. Bishop JP, who was now the Mayor of Folkestone.

There were literally hundreds of wreaths and other floral displays laid at the base of the memorial by different groups and organisations wishing to pay their respects to the fallen men of the town.

Colonel W.J. Duggan of the Shorncliffe Garrison was present, as was the Deputy Mayor of Calais, as well as the French, Belgian and Italian Vice Consuls. There were not many memorials in Britain that could boast a guest list of such cosmopolitan and high-ranking individuals at their unveiling ceremonies. There were also, of course, the relatives of those who had died, ex-servicemen, and those had been friends and colleagues of the dead. Landed gentry and common man stood side by side in packed crowds for as far as the eye could see.

A guard of honour was provided from the Oxfordshire and Buckinghamshire Light Infantry, under the command of Lieutenant Colonel F.H. Stapleton CMG. A lieutenant held the battalion's colours and two sergeant majors were posted in front of the memorial. Behind the officers and men from the Oxfordshire and Buckinghamshire Light Infantry, who also provided their band and buglers, was a contingent of RAF personnel from 56th Squadron, under the command of Squadron Leader R.T. Lloyd. Others included 4th Battalion, the Buffs, and the Royal Field Artillery.

Also in attendance were groups of girl guides, boy scouts, sea scouts, HM Coastguard, nurses, the Voluntary Aid Detachment (under the watchful eye of Mrs Moule), Folkestone Fire Brigade, the local police, Captain H.O. Jones from Folkestone Harbour, as well as a detachment from the St John Ambulance. There were even representatives from the Ancient Order of Druids, the Ancient Order of Foresters, and the Royal Antediluvian Order of Buffaloes. There was a choir of some 200 children present from the nearby Sidney Street school, who were dutifully led by the school's headmaster, Mr Percy Greenstreet.

The memorial is 25 feet high and 26 feet wide, is made out of

Cornish granite, and is topped with a bronze female figurine that carries a cross in one hand and a laurel wreath in the other. The inscription reads:

Thanks be to God who giveth us the victory in every grateful memory of the brave men from Folkestone, and the many thousands from all parts of the Empire who passed this spot on their way to fight in the Great War (1914-1918) for righteousness and freedom, and especially those of this town who made the supreme sacrifice, and whose names are hereby recorded, this memorial is humbly dedicated.

There are 578 names on the memorial:

Adair-Hall, Malcolm W F, Lieutenant, Royal Inniskilling Fusiliers
Allchin, Stephen L, Private, Lincolnshire Regiment
Allen, George F, Private, the Buffs (East Kent Regiment)
Allen, George W, Private, Essex Regiment
Allen, Thomas H, Private, the Buffs (East Kent Regiment)
Allen, Thomas J, Able Seaman, Royal Naval Reserve
Alsop, William C P, Sergeant, London Regiment
Ames, Albert R, Private, the Buffs (East Kent Regiment)
Ames, Ivan W, Lieutenant, Queen's Own Royal West Kent
Ames, Robert H, Captain, Leicestershire Regiment
Ames, William K, Lieutenant, Queen's Own Royal West Kent
Amos, Edward H, Private, the Buffs (East Kent Regiment)
Amos, Percy B, Rifleman, London Regiment
Amos, Vic, Signaller, London Regiment
Anderson, Charles, Driver, Royal Army Service Corps
Anderson, William, Private, the Buffs (East Kent Regiment)
Andrews, Alfred, 1st Class Stoker, Royal Naval Reserve
Andrews, Charles J, Lance Corporal, Queen's Own Royal West Kent
Andrews, Percy A, Private, Royal Fusiliers
Andrews, Thomas, Private, the Buffs (East Kent Regiment)
Angus, John, Company Sergeant Major, Royal Scots
Appleton, Thomas E, Lance Corporal, the Buffs (East Kent Regiment)
Archer, Harry, Private, Australian Imperial Forces
Argar, Albert G, Private, Kent Cyclist Battalion
Argar, Dudley J, Gunner, Royal Field Artillery
Argar, Stephen H, Driver, Royal Field Artillery
Armstrong, W M, Lieutenant, 11th Hussars
Arnold, Archibald H, Driver, Royal Field Artillery
Arthur, William N, Private, the Buffs (East Kent Regiment)

Ashdown, Edward E, Bugler, London Regiment
Ashman, Charles E, Lance Sergeant, Royal Marines
Aspinall, Robert L, Lieutenant Colonel, Cheshire Regiment
Attwood, Maurice L, Private, Canadian Expeditionary Force
Austin, Alfred J, Private, East Yorkshire Regiment
Avis, William A, Private, London Regiment
Bailey, Albert E, Gunner, Royal Garrison Artillery
Bailey, Charles V, Private, Royal Fusiliers
Bailey, Christopher G W, Private, Essex Regiment
Bailey, Edward W, Lance Corporal, Royal Engineers
Baker, Frank, Sergeant, Royal Army Service Corps
Baker, George F, Private, the Buffs (East Kent Regiment)
Baker, Harry C, Captain, Canadian Expeditionary Force
Baker, Joseph C, Private, Sherwood Foresters
Baker, Montague, Private, Royal Berkshire Regiment
Baldock, George W, Rifleman, London Regiment
Banks, Walter W, CQMS, the Buffs (East Kent Regiment)
Banting, Henry H, Private, the Buffs (East Kent Regiment)
Barden, Edward G, Lance Corporal, the Buffs (East Kent Regiment)
Barker, Godfrey, Major, Royal Marines
Barranger, George, Private, the Buffs (East Kent Regiment)
Barrett, Cecil R, 2nd Lieutenant, Royal Field Artillery
Barrett, Robert, Private, Royal Fusiliers
Barron, Leslie, 2nd Lieutenant, Royal Air Force
Barton, Arthur O, Private, Queen's Royal Regiment West Surrey
Barton, David, Private, Australian Imperial Forces
Barton, Edward, Able Seaman, Royal Naval Reserve
Bates, Albert H, Corporal, Canadian Expeditionary Force
Beldon, James, Rifleman, King's Royal Rifle Corps
Bell, William J, Leading Seaman, Royal Naval Reserve
Berridge, W E, 2nd Lieutenant, Somerset Light Infantry
Binfield, Herbert, Rifleman, London Regiment
Binfield, Joseph, Gunner, Royal Garrison Artillery
Birch, George M, Private, Royal Army Service Corps
Black, Louis, Corporal, Kent Cyclist Battalion
Blackall, Charles W, Lieutenant Colonel, South Staffordshire Regiment
Bloge, Charles C, Driver, Royal Garrison Artillery
Bodker, John G, Lieutenant, Duke of Wellington's Regiment West Riding
Boland, Harold G W, Lance Corporal, Prince of Wales's Volunteers
Borthwick, Arthur P S, 2nd Lieutenant, Machine Gun Corps
Bosher, George T, Private, Machine Gun Corps

Bowe, George J, Private, the Buffs (East Kent Regiment)
Brann, William E, Able Seaman, Royal Naval Reserve
Brice, James G, Private, London Regiment
Bridger, Alexander W J, Private, Royal Warwickshire Regiment
Bridges, Frederick J, Private, Royal Sussex Regiment
Brine, F Ronald, Corporal, Machine Gun Corps
Brockway, George, Staff Sergeant, 13th Hussars
Bromley, Harold, Private, London Regiment
Bromley, William, Private, Australian Imperial Forces
Bull, Albert, 1st Class Petty Officer, Royal Naval Reserve
Bull, Harold J, Sergeant, Australian Imperial Army
Bull, Thomas, Sergeant, Australian Imperial Army
Bunce, Herbert W, Corporal, Royal Army Service Corps
Burrows, Albert E, Chief Petty Officer, Royal Naval Reserve
Burrows, Fred, Private, the Buffs (East Kent Regiment)
Burstowe, Horace W, Gunner, Royal Garrison Artillery
Bushell, Arthur, Corporal, York and Lancashire Regiment
Butcher, Frederick C, Private, the Buffs (East Kent Regiment)
Butler, Henry G, Private, Queen's Royal West Surrey Regiment
Byrne, Arthur T, Lance Corporal, Oxford & Bucks Light Infantry
Camburn, George H, Private, North Staffordshire Regiment
Campbell, Montague I M, Major, Connaught Rangers
Campion, George, Sergeant, Highland Light Infantry
Cann, Leopold V M, Sergeant, Royal Army Service Corps
Carswell, Charles, Private, Welch Regiment
Carter, George R, Private, Royal Army Medical Corps
Catt, Alfred E, Private, the Buffs (East Kent Regiment)
Catt, Edward P, Able Seaman, Royal Naval Reserve
Chalcraft, Walter C, Private, Queen's Royal West Surrey
Charingbold, William H, Private, Machine Gun Corps
Chidwick, Alfred J, Private, Royal Munster Fusiliers
Chidwick, Arthur E, Private, Highland Light Infantry
Childs, Charles, Private, Machine Gun Corps
Claringbould, Frederick W, Private, the Buffs (East Kent Regiment)
Clark, Charles V, Gunner, Royal Field Artillery
Clark, Henry G, Private, the Buffs (East Kent Regiment)
Clark, John W F, Guardsman, Grenadier Guards
Clarke, Robert S, Private, Queen's Own Royal West Kent
Clayton, Victor A, Private, Queen's Own Royal West Kent
Cloake, Stephen J H, Trooper, 3rd Hussars
Cloke, Sydney D, Rifleman, London Regiment

Cobb, Sydney J, 2nd Lieutenant, Royal Munster Fusiliers
Cocks Thomas F, Lance Corporal, Kent Cyclist Battalion
Coleman, Francis, Rifleman, King's Royal Rifle Corps
Coleman, James, Private, the Buffs (East Kent Regiment)
Collier, Sidney A P, Corporal, Devonshire Regiment
Collins, Lancelot R, Staff Sergeant Major, Royal Field Artillery
Coombes, Percy H, Private, Royal Fusiliers
Cornish, Zachariah, Mooring Hand, Royal Naval Reserve
Cottrell, John P, 2nd Lieutenant, Queen's Own Royal West Kent
Coughlan, Daniel J A, Chief Steward, Royal Naval Reserve
Court, Frank D, Lance Corporal, the Buffs (East Kent Regiment)
Court, John S S, Private, the Buffs (East Kent Regiment)
Court, Stephen C, Corporal, King's Regiment (Liverpool)
Cox, Harry, Able Seaman, Royal Naval Reserve
Cox, Philip W, Bombardier, Royal Field Artillery
Craft, Harry A, Lance Corporal, London Regiment
Cramer-Roberts, Edward H, 2nd Lieutenant, the Buffs (East Kent
    Regiment)
Croucher, Frederick W, Private, Queen's Own Royal West Kent
Cryer, Ernest, 46th Battalion, Australian Imperial Forces
Cullen, John, Gunner, Royal Garrison Artillery
Cullum, Harold, Private, Royal Fusiliers
Curragh, Emerson, Private, Middlesex Regiment
Curtin, Joseph T, Private, North Staffordshire Regiment
Curtis, Archibald R, Sergeant, Royal Army Medical Corps
de Satge, Frederick G, Captain, King's Royal Rifle Corps
Denne, Richard A, Private, Queen's Own Royal West Kent
Dilnot, Lewis, Cook, Royal Naval Reserve
Dodge, Arthur W, Driver, Royal Field Artillery
Dolby, Lionel R, Sapper, Royal Engineers
Dorrill, Walter E, Corporal, Ox & Bucks Light Infantry
Doughty, Frederick J, Gunner, Royal Field Artillery
Down, Frederick C, Sapper, Royal Engineers
Doyle, Arthur J, Private, Hampshire Regiment
Drake-Brockman Paris V, 2nd Lieutenant, the Buffs (East Kent
    Regiment)
Drake-Brockman, Ralph, 2nd Lieutenant, Royal Field Artillery
Dray, Edward T, Stoker, Royal Naval Reserve
Duggan, Richard H J, Corporal, Canadian Infantry
Duke, Barry T, Lieutenant, Royal Sussex Regiment
Duncan, Arthur J, Corporal, Royal Army Service Corps

Duncan, Charles E, Corporal, Rifle Brigade
Duncombe, Walter J, Private, Royal Army Medical Corps
Edwards, A Corbett, Captain, Queen's Own Royal West Kent
Edwards, Frederick H, Private, East Surrey Regiment
Eldridge, Theodore T S, Private, Royal East Kent Yeomanry
Elgar, Edward W E, Private, the Buffs (East Kent Regiment)
Elgar, Ernest J, Lance Corporal, Royal Fusiliers
Ellen, Arthur C, Lieutenant, Royal Garrison Artillery
Ellis, George C, Private, the Buffs (East Kent Regiment)
English, Nathaniel J, Captain, Royal Naval Reserve
Evans, Ernest, 2nd Lieutenant, Royal Garrison Artillery
Evans, John H, 1st Class Petty Officer, Royal Naval Reserve
Everson, Richard H, Private, the Buffs (East Kent Regiment)
Fagg, Richard W, Private, Worcestershire Regiment
Faggetter, William A, Trooper, 9th Lancers
Farley, Ernest, Lance Corporal, Canadian Infantry
Feather, Reginald A, Lieutenant, Hampshire Regiment
Featherbe, Alfred, Gunner, Royal Field Artillery
Feist, Gordon, Private, the Buffs (East Kent Regiment)
Fennell, John T, Chief Petty Officer, Royal Naval Reserve
Finn, Frederick W, Private, Queen's Own Royal West Kent
Finn, Walter H, Private, Royal Fusiliers
Fletcher, Stanley K G, Lance Corporal, Machine Gun Corps
Flisher, Harold S, Private, the Buffs (East Kent Regiment)
Ford, Frederick H, Sapper, Royal Engineers
Ford, William A, Sapper, Royal Engineers
Foreman, Victor, Private, Middlesex Regiment
Fowler, Harold, Trooper, County of London Yeomanry
Francis, Arthur E, Lance Corporal, Queen's Royal (West Surrey)
    Regiment
Francis, Frank W, Lance Corporal, New Zealand Forces
Francis, William W, Private, the Buffs (East Kent Regiment)
Fray, Percy E, Lance Corporal, the Buffs (East Kent Regiment)
French, William J, Private, Loyal Regiment (North Lancashire)
French, Noel, Sapper, Royal Engineers
Frost, Charles D, Captain, Indian Army
Fullard, Arthur D, Private, London Regiment
Furnival, Edward H, Driver, Royal Field Artillery
Gains, Albert F, Lance Corporal, London Regiment
Gains, Arthur E, Rifleman, King's Royal Rifle Corps
Garlinge, Ernest E, Private, the Buffs (East Kent Regiment)

Gibbs, E F, Private, Canadian Expeditionary Force
Gibson, Thomas J, Private, East Surrey Regiment
Gifford, Aubrey W, Private, Australian Imperial Forces
Gilbertson, Dennis H S, Lieutenant, Royal Air Force
Gilham, Leonard F, Corporal, Highland Light Infantry
Goddard, Archibald S, Captain, Canadian Infantry
Godfrey, Jack P, Private, London Regiment
Golden, Frank C A, Lieutenant, Durham Light Infantry
Golder, Frederick J, Private, Northamptonshire Regiment
Goldsack, Stephen E, Private, East Surrey Regiment
Goodburn, Edward, Signaller, Ox & Bucks Light Infantry
Goodenough, John, Private, Essex Regiment
Goodman, Frederick J, Private, Machine Gun Corps
Gore, Sydney K, Lieutenant, Queen's Own Royal West Kent
Grace, Walter G, Boy Mechanic, Royal Air Force
Green, Harry E, Driver, Royal Field Artillery
Greengrass, Charles F, Able Seaman, Royal Naval Reserve
Greenland, Frank, Private, Royal Army Medical Corps
Greenland, Frederick J, Able Seaman, Royal Naval Reserve
Griffin, Clive, Lieutenant, Royal Field Artillery
Grinstead, Solomon, Private, Royal Sussex Regiment
Gye, Alex H, Lieutenant Commander, Royal Naval Reserve
Hadaway, C Henry, Private, Middlesex Regiment
Hall, Bertie W, Private, Seaforth Highlanders
Hall, Fred A, Private, East Surrey Regiment
Hall, Frederick, Private, the Buffs (East Kent Regiment)
Hall, George, Deck Hand, Royal Naval Reserve
Hall, Henry, Mooring Hand, Royal Naval Reserve
Hall, Thomas C, Private, London Regiment
Hall, William A, Private, the Buffs (East Kent Regiment)
Hammond, Sidney C, Private, Queen's Own Royal West Kent
Handford, Ernest M, Private, London Regiment
Hannon, Michael N, Private, the Buffs (East Kent Regiment)
Hardiman, William C, Sergeant, Royal East Kent Yeomanry
Hare, Harry V, Captain, Durham Light Infantry
Harris, George W, Private, Royal Munster Fusiliers
Harris, William J, Deck Hand, Royal Naval Reserve
Harris, William T, Private, Prince of Wales' Volunteers
Harrison, George, Sergeant, Grenadier Guards
Harrison, Robert G, Lance Corporal, the Buffs (East Kent Regiment)
Hart, Charles, Private, the Buffs (East Kent Regiment)

Hastie, Frederick, CSM, Devonshire Regiment
Hatfield, Salisbury, Private, Australian Imperial Forces
Hathorn, George H V, Lieutenant, Royal Marines
Hathorn, Noel McD, 2nd Lieutenant, Indian Army
Haydon, Thomas, Private, Royal Army Medical Corps
Hayes, Archibald, Trooper, 14th Hussars
Haywood, George H, Private, the Buffs (East Kent Regiment)
Head, James, Private, Royal Fusiliers
Henley, Alfred, Chief Petty Officer, Royal Naval Reserve
Herd, Ernest W, Sergeant, Royal Army Service Corps
Heritage, William R, Private, Middlesex Regiment
Heydon, G W Cyril, 2nd Class Air Mechanic, Royal Air Force
Hilder, William, Sergeant, Royal Army Medical Corps
Hill, Harry R, Private, Queen's Royal Regiment (West Surrey)
Hills, Harry W, Private, the Buffs (East Kent Regiment)
Hogben, George F, Private, Prince of Wales's Volunteers
Hogben, Lawrence, Private, Queen's Own Royal West Kent
Hogben, Theophilus, Sergeant, Royal Garrison Artillery
Hogben, Thomas, Gunner, Royal Field Artillery
Hollamby, Edward H, Telegraphist, Royal Naval Reserve
Holland, Francis J, Able Seaman, Royal Naval Reserve
Holtum, George A, Private, Royal Army Medical Corps
Hook, Harry, Gunner, Royal Field Artillery
Hoper, Abraham, Sergeant, Queen's Own Royal West Kent
Hopkins, Thomas K, Private, Beds and Herts Regiment
Hoskyns, Henry C W, Major, Lincolnshire Regiment
Hounsom, Albert G H, Sergeant, Royal Sussex Regiment
Howard, William E, Private, Somerset Light Infantry
Hughes, Norman, Private, Royal Fusiliers
Hughes, William L, Able Seaman, Royal Naval Reserve
Hunter, William, CSM, Highland Light Infantry
Impett, John, Private, Leicestershire Regiment
Innes, William G, Private, Royal Army Service Corps
Jago, George J, Private, Gloucestershire Regiment
Jarvis, William E, Corporal, Royal Warwickshire Regiment
Johnson, William, Lance Corporal, the Buffs (East Kent Regiment)
Johnson, William H G, Private, Royal Army Service Corps
Jones, Edward O, Lance Corporal, Gloucestershire Yeomanry
Jones, F Walwyn, Gunner, Royal Field Artillery
Jones, Robert C, Private, London Regiment
Jones, Samuel G A, Sergeant, Grenadier Guards

Jones, W, CQMS, Royal Warwickshire Regiment
Keeler, Frederick P, Private, the Buffs (East Kent Regiment)
Keeling, Arthur R, Corporal, Royal Fusiliers
Kemp, Jesse, Private, the Buffs (East Kent Regiment)
Kennedy, Albert G H, Private, Queen's Royal West Surrey
Kennett, George A, Private, Canadian Expeditionary Force
Kennett, Thomas, Lance Corporal, the Buffs (East Kent Regiment)
King, Albert, Private, Northumberland Fusiliers
Kingsbury, Jesse H, Private, Canadian Expeditionary Force
Kingsley, Charles E, Sergeant, Canadian Infantry
Knight, William L, Lance Corporal, Royal Fusiliers
Lake, James A, Lance Corporal, the Buffs (East Kent Regiment)
Lake, Joseph D, Private, Queen's Royal Regiment (West Surrey)
Lamb, Harold G W, 2nd Lieutenant, Royal Fusiliers
Lambert, Gilbert J, Ordinary Telegraphist, Royal Naval Reserve
Lambert, Jack F, 2nd Lieutenant, King's Royal Rifle Corps
Laney, John, Lance Sergeant, Canadian Infantry
Larkin, Charles H, Private, Norfolk Regiment
Laws, Robert H, Corporal, the Buffs (East Kent Regiment)
Lea, George, Rifleman, King's Royal Rifle Corps
Lee, Percy J A B, Royal Naval Reserve
Legg, Frederick C, Sergeant, London Regiment
Lemar, Charles P, Private, Loyal Regiment (North Lancs)
Lemar, Frederick, Private, Loyal Regiment (North Lancs)
Linkin, Percy G, Private, Royal Marines
Longley, William H, Private, the Buffs (East Kent Regiment)
Lord, William A, 2nd Class Petty Officer, Royal Naval Reserve
Low, Eustace B, 2nd Lieutenant, Royal Air Force
Mace, Henry O, Private, Queen's Own Royal West Kent
Maire, Walter, Able Seaman, Royal Naval Reserve
Major, Donald, Sergeant, Canadian Infantry
Major, Henry W, Private, Queen's Royal (West Surrey) Reg
Major, Roland, Sergeant, Canadian Infantry
Male, William, 1st Class Stoker, Royal Naval Reserve
Manning, James, Private, the Buffs (East Kent Regiment)
Manning, William, Private, the Buffs (East Kent Regiment)
Mant, Walter J J, QMS, Royal Army Medical Corps
Maplesden, Wilfred J, Private, Beds and Herts Regiment
Mardle, Herbert W, Bombardier, Royal Field Artillery
Marsh, Arthur J, Corporal, Royal Engineers
Marsh, George B, Sergeant, Royal Field Artillery

Marsh, Thomas J A B, Royal Naval Reserve
Marsh, Walter, Private, Royal Inniskilling Fusiliers
Marsh, William S, Private, Queen's Own Royal West Kent
Marshall, Frank, Private, Royal Sussex Regiment
Marwood, William G, Seaman, Royal Naval Reserve
Marwood, Charles P L, Captain, Royal Warwickshire Regiment
Maxted, Archibald, Private, Dorsetshire Regiment
Maxted, Percy E, Gunner, Royal Field Artillery
May, Joseph, Private, East Yorkshire Regiment
May, William J, Corporal, Prince of Wales' Leinster Regiment
McPartlin, William, Sergeant, Royal Field Artillery
McWilliams, Victor J, Private, the Buffs (East Kent Regiment)
Meath, Thomas W, Lance Corporal, Gloucestershire Regiment
Menzies, William A, 2nd Lieutenant, Royal Garrison Artillery
Mepsted, Archie, Lance Corporal, Grenadier Guards
Miles, John, Mooring Hand, Royal Naval Reserve
Millen, Leslie F, Private, Royal Army Service Corps
Mills, Cyril, Corporal, Queen's Royal Regiment (West Surrey)
Mills, James W, Private, Bedfordshire and Hertfordshire Reg
Milton, Frederick, Private, the Buffs (East Kent Regiment)
Milton, Henry T, Lance Corporal, the Buffs (East Kent Regiment)
Milton, Horace A, 1st Class Stoker, Royal Naval Reserve
Milton, Leonard, Private, the Buffs (East Kent Regiment)
Minter, George H, Private, Royal Army Medical Corps
Moat, Ephraim G A B, Royal Naval Reserve
Moat, Walter J, 2nd Class Petty Officer Royal Naval Reserve
Moore, George H, Able Seaman, Royal Naval Reserve
Moore, Herbert D, Private, Royal Fusiliers
Muir, John H, Major, 17th Lancers
Mullett, Arthur, Private, the Buffs (East Kent Regiment)
Mullett, George, Rifleman, King's Royal Rifle Corps
Mullett, William H, Private, Middlesex Regiment
Mummery, Arthur, Stoker Petty Officer, Royal Naval Reserve
Munday, Charles E, Private, Queen's Royal (West Surrey) Reg
Munday, William T, Rifleman, King's Royal Rifle Corps
Murphy, John C M, Bugler, Royal Marines
Musgrave, John, Lance Corporal, South Staffordshire Regiment
Myers, Henry J, Captain, Royal Army Service Corps
Nesbit, Henry G, Lieutenant, the Buffs (East Kent Regiment)
Newman, Archie V, Rifleman, London Regiment
Newman, Percy B, Driver, Royal Engineers

Newman, Reginald G, Trooper, Royal East Kent Yeomanry
Newman, William, Corporal, Royal Fusiliers
Nicholson, John E P, 2nd Lieutenant, Loyal Regiment (North Lancashire)
Noble, James R, Deck Hand, Royal Naval Reserve
Norrington, William, Private, Durham Light Infantry
Norris, Herbert, Captain, Canadian Expeditionary Force
Noyes, Charles H C, Sergeant, Observer Royal Air Force
Nutley, Frederick E, Lance Corporal, the Buffs (East Kent Regiment)
O'Leary, Frederick T, Private, Royal Fusiliers
Ongley, Arthur F, Private, Royal Army Service Corps
Orchard, Alfred H, Royal Naval Reserve
Orchard, Sidney G, Private, Queen's Royal (West Surrey)
Ovenden, Frederick, Gunner, Royal Field Artillery
Page, Frederick H, Stoker, Petty Officer Royal Naval Reserve
Page, Reginald P, CSM, Norfolk Regiment
Page, Stanley W, Gunner, Royal Garrison Artillery
Page, Walter P, Private, Royal Army Service Corps
Paine, Charles, Private, Beds and Herts Regiment
Palmer, Charles E, Private, Royal Marines Light Infantry
Palmer, John, Private, the Buffs (East Kent Regiment)
Pankhurst, Alfred J, Corporal, Canadian Infantry
Parker, Robert C W, Private, the Buffs (East Kent Regiment)
Parks, George C, Private, Royal Marines Light Infantry
Parsons, Alfred H, Captain, Indian Army
Pegden, Redvers G B, Private, the Buffs (East Kent Regiment)
Pegg, Frederick R, Private, Royal Army Service Corps
Penfold, Jeffery B, Lieutenant, King's Own Scottish Borderers
Penny, F, Private, Royal Fusiliers
Peters, Frederick G, Rifleman, Rifle Brigade
Peters, William H, Private, Royal Sussex Regiment
Pettman, Archibald L, Private, the Buffs (East Kent Regiment)
Petty, John E, Sergeant, Royal Field Artillery
Philpott, George, Corporal, the Buffs (East Kent Regiment)
Philpott, James, Private, Queen's Royal Regiment (West Surrey)
Philpott, Thomas B, Lance Corporal, Rifle Brigade
Piddock, Leonard, Corporal, Border Regiment
Pilcher, Alfred M, Lieutenant, London Regiment
Pilcher, Denzil T, Private, Machine Gun Corps
Pilcher, Henry J, Sergeant, Royal East Kent Yeomanry
Piper, Harry A, Private, Suffolk Regiment
Piper, Herbert, Private, Queen's Own Royal West Kent

Pittock, Sidney T, Private, Middlesex Regiment
Plaistowe, Frederick H, Sapper, Royal Engineers
Poile, William F, Private, Royal Fusiliers
Polden, Alfred, Private, Northumberland Fusiliers
Pollard, William S, Private, Royal Army Medical Corps
Poole, Frederick D, Private, Royal Army Medical Corps
Poole, Herbert E W, Private, the Buffs (East Kent Regiment)
Portch, Henry C, Private, Manchester Regiment
Porter, Bert, Private, London Regiment
Porter, Harold E, Private, London Regiment
Prior, William, Private, Middlesex Regiment
Puttee, Arthur A, Lance Corporal, London Regiment
Quaife, Henry, Private, the Buffs (East Kent Regiment)
Quaife, Robert W W, Private, the Buffs (East Kent Regiment)
Quinn, William J, Lance Corporal, Machine Gun Corps
Rawlinson, Frederick E V, Private, Royal Fusiliers
Rayner, Ernest A C, Private, Northamptonshire Regiment
Rayner, George, Private, the Buffs (East Kent Regiment)
Reader, Horace W, Private, the Buffs (East Kent Regiment)
Reeve, Harry, 2nd Lieutenant, King's Regiment (Liverpool)
Reynolds-Peyton, John, Lieutenant, Royal Naval Reserve
Richards, Charles E, Private, the Buffs (East Kent Regiment)
Richards, William R, Bandsman, Suffolk Regiment
Richardson, Henry, Sub-Lieutenant Royal Naval Reserve
Richardson, Henry D, Private, East Surrey Regiment
Richardson, Ronald, Private, King's Own Yorkshire Light Infantry
Rickaby, Maurice C, Lance Corporal, King's Royal Rifle Corps
Ridgeway, Theophilus, Lance Corporal, Manchester Regiment
Ridsdale, Robert H, Signaller, Canadian Infantry
Ripley, Charles R, 2nd Lieutenant, York and Lancaster Regiment
Roberts, Cyril H, Private, the Buffs (East Kent Regiment)
Robinson, Charles L, Private, Welch Regiment
Robus, Frederick J, Deck Hand, Royal Naval Reserve
Robus, Thomas J, Sapper, Royal Engineers
Rolfe, Alfred, Private, the Buffs (East Kent Regiment)
Rose, John, Private, Middlesex Regiment
Rumney, Charles, Private, the Buffs (East Kent Regiment)
Rumsey, Frederick G, Corporal, Royal Fusiliers
Ryan, Thomas, Private, the Buffs (East Kent Regiment)
Rye, Edward, Private, the Buffs (East Kent Regiment)
Rye, George, Private, Australian Imperial Forces

Rye, James, Private, Queen's Royal Regiment (West Surrey)
Salter, Charles E, Private, the Buffs (East Kent Regiment)
Sankey, Thomas, Captain, West Yorkshire Regiment
Saunders, Albert J, Private, Queen's Own Royal West Kent
Saunders, Clifford W, Captain, Dorsetshire Regiment
Saunders, Walter G, Private, Royal Warwickshire Regiment
Savage, Fred, Private, the Buffs (East Kent Regiment)
Savage, Herbert E, Private, Royal Army Service Corps
Scott, George F, Private, the Buffs (East Kent Regiment)
Seales, William H, Corporal, Norfolk Regiment
Setterfield, Edward, Private, the Buffs (East Kent Regiment)
Seymour, Vere, Lieutenant, Royal Naval Reserve
Shaw, Edwin R, Sergeant, Royal Army Service Corps
Shaw, John, Lieutenant, Canadian Infantry
Sherwood, Cyril E, Corporal, the Buffs (East Kent Regiment)
Shopland, Edward J, Private, Queen's Own Royal West Kent
Short, Vere D, Captain, Northamptonshire Regiment
Shrubsole, William J, Sergeant, the Buffs (East Kent Regiment)
Sidey, Ernest R, Lance Corporal, Royal Irish Rifles
Silvester, William H, Warrant Telegraphist, Royal Naval Reserve
Simpson, Ernest K, Able Seaman, Royal Naval Reserve
Simpson, William E, Private, the Buffs (East Kent Regiment)
Skeet, George V, Private, Queen's Royal (West Surrey) Reg
Skerritt, Edward J, Private, Australian Imperial Forces
Smart, Eustace F, Lieutenant, Leicestershire Regiment
Smith, George, Corporal, Australian Imperial Forces
Smith, Sidney M, Private, the Buffs (East Kent Regiment)
Southon, Walter C, 1st Class Petty Officer, Royal Naval Reserve
Spearpoint, James, Private, Canadian Infantry
Spearpoint, William, Private, the Buffs (East Kent Regiment)
Spendlove, William C, Air Mechanic 2nd Class, Royal Flying Corps
Spickett, Robert A, Private, Queen's Royal (West Surrey)
Standing, Thomas R, Sergeant, Queen's Own Royal West Kent
Standing, Thomas W, Able Seaman, Royal Naval Reserve
Stanfield, Cecil, Captain, the Buffs (East Kent) Regiment
Stay, Henry R, Trooper, Royal East Kent Yeomanry
Stephens, Samuel, Sergeant, Royal Field Artillery
Stevens, Albert, Corporal, Royal Warwickshire Regiment
Stokes, Arthur C, Private, Royal Fusiliers
Stokes, Charles L, Pioneer, Royal Engineers
Stokes, Frederick, Private, London Regiment

Stokes, Walter H, Private, Royal Fusiliers
Streatfield, Thomas B M, 2nd Lieutenant, Queen's Own Royal West Kent
Strood, Percy S, Lieutenant, Canadian Infantry
Strutts, Henniker W, Trooper, 20th Hussars
Summerfield, Jack, Private, Queen's Royal Regiment (West Surrey)
Summers, Frederick J, Private, Royal Army Ordnance Corps
Swain, Leslie, Corporal, Canadian Infantry
Swift, Cecil H, Private, East Yorkshire Regiment
Swift, George K, Gunner, Royal Garrison Artillery
Taylor, David G, Seaman, Royal Naval Reserve
Taylor, Frederick C, 2nd Lieutenant, Royal Air Force
Taylor, Frederick J, Private, the Buffs (East Kent Regiment)
Taylor, Frederick J, Seaman, Royal Naval Reserve
Taylor, George, Private, Queen's Own Royal West Kent
Taylor, Hugh, Corporal, the Buffs (East Kent Regiment)
Taylor, John W, Private, Royal Fusiliers
Taylor, Thomas H, Private, Royal Marines
Thomas, William B, Sergeant, Royal Army Medical Corps
Thompson, William E, Rifleman, Rifle Brigade
Thomson, Alfred, Private, the Buffs (East Kent Regiment)
Thornbee, Cecil, Private, Machine Gun Corps
Thurlow, John W, Private, London Regiment
Tiddy, John, Guardsman, Grenadier Guards
Tooth, Sitnah J, Corporal, Royal Field Artillery
Tribe, Ernest H, Private, Middlesex Regiment
Trice, Franklyn R, Sergeant, Royal Fusiliers
Tritton, Cecil J, Private, the Buffs (East Kent Regiment)
Tuffex Charles J, Able Seaman, Royal Naval Reserve
Tull, Walter D, 2nd Lieutenant, Middlesex Regiment
Tumber, Victor J, Seaman, Royal Naval Reserve
Tupper, Ernest, Stoker Petty Officer, Royal Naval Reserve
Turner, Edwin, Private, Canadian Infantry
Tutt, George W, Lance Corporal, the Buffs (East Kent Regiment)
Tutt, Stephen C, Corporal, Queen's Royal Regiment (West Surrey)
Upton, Philip C, Sergeant, the Buffs (East Kent Regiment)
Upton, William G, Sergeant, Machine Gun Corps
Varney John W L, Signaller, Royal Naval Reserve
Vinnicombe, Harry V, Private, Australian Infantry
Vinnicombe, L, Lieutenant, Devonshire Regiment
Waddell, John A, Private, Beds and Herts Regiment
Waddell, William G, Private, Royal Fusiliers

Wainwright, Geoffrey L, 2nd Lieutenant, Royal Sussex Regiment
Walder, George, 1st Class Stoker, Royal Naval Reserve
Walter, Frank, Sapper, Royal Engineers
Walter, William F, Major, Lancashire Fusiliers
Wampach, Alfred, Driver, Royal Field Artillery
Warman, William R H, Private, the Buffs (East Kent Reg)
Webb, John M, Corporal, London Regiment
Webster, Clement C, Lance Corporal, the Buffs (East Kent Regiment)
Weller, Alfred J, Sergeant, Canadian Infantry
Weller, Sidney, Lance Sergeant, Grenadier Guards
Welsh, William E N, Stoker Petty Officer, Royal Naval Reserve
Whitehead, Archibald, Corporal, Royal Army Service Corps
Whiting, Charles H, Private, the Buffs (East Kent Regiment)
Whittall, Garth, 2nd Lieutenant, Royal Air Force
Wildsmith, Raymond C, Lieutenant, London Regiment
Wilkinson, R Bruce, 2nd Lieutenant, Loyal Regiment (North Lancashire)
Williams, Arthur I, Sergeant, Royal Army Medical Corps
Williams, George, Private, the Buffs (East Kent Regiment)
Williams, Henry G, Private, Canadian Infantry
Willis, Alfred, Driver, Royal Field Artillery
Willis, Frank E, Sapper, Royal Engineers
Willis, Thomas J, Sergeant, Royal Field Artillery
Willis. William H, Driver, Royal Field Artillery
Wills, John E, Private, Royal Fusiliers
Willson, P, Lieutenant Major, Canadian Infantry
Wilson, Alfred, Sergeant, King's Royal Rifle Corps
Winchester, William S, Private, the Buffs (East Kent Regiment)
Winchurst, Frederick W, Private, East Surrey Regiment
Winder, Cecil, Private, the Buffs (East Kent Regiment)
Winterton, Harold, Rifleman, London Regiment
Winton, Albert E, Able Seaman, Royal Naval Reserve
Wise, Frederick S, Able Seaman, Royal Naval Reserve
Witch, Percy C, Private, the Buffs (East Kent Regiment)
Wollett, George, Private, Queen's Royal Regiment (West Surrey)
Wolsey, Philip, CQM Sergeant, Royal East Kent Yeomanry
Wood, Alfred, Sergeant, the Buffs (East Kent Regiment)
Wood, Reginald E, 2nd Lieutenant, the Buffs (East Kent Regiment)
Woods, Maurice J, Able Seaman, Royal Naval Reserve
Woods, Wilfred H, Stoker Petty Officer, Royal Naval Reserve
Woollett, Walter, Guardsman, Grenadier Guards
Wooton, James F, Able Seaman, Royal Naval Reserve

Wraight, Horace, Gunner, Royal Field Artillery
Wraight, Leslie C, 2nd Lieutenant, Royal Air Force
Wright, Charles S, Rifleman, King's Royal Rifle Corps
Wright, Harry, Second Hand, Royal Naval Reserve
Wright, William L, Sapper, Royal Engineers
Wyatt, George A, Lance Corporal, the Buffs (East Kent Regiment)
Wyborn, Norman W A, Private, Queen's Own Royal West Kent
Wyborn, Robert W, Private, the Buffs (East Kent Regiment)
Youden, Alfred C, Gunner, Royal Field Artillery
Young, William G, Gunner, Royal Garrison Artillery

During the war a total of forty-five men of the 1st/4th Battalion, East
Kent (The Buffs) Regiment were killed or died of their injuries. They
are recorded below, in the date order that they died:

Private TF/2181 John Wayte. Died 19/2/1915.
Bandsman 1663 Thomas Goodwin. Died 12/7/1915.
Private T/2167 Richard Richardson. Died 21/9/1915.
Sergeant 337 W T Brazier. Died 25/9/1915.
Private 2330 William Edward Bromley. Died 25/9/1915.
Private 1940 G R Brown. Died 25/9/1915.
Private 2334 H R De la Mare. Died 25/9/1915.
Private 2073 Lionel Henry Fuller. Died 25/9/1915.
Private 2205 W R Maslin. Died 25/9/1915.
Sergeant T/504 Edward George Dyer. Died 25/9/1915.
Lance Corporal 176. Percy James Lawford. Died 30/5/1916.
Private T/2013 Charles Albert Martin. Died 25/8/1916.
Private 4511 Gilbert William. Died 23/9/1916.
Captain Victor Arnold. Died 15/1/1917.
CQMS 200524 William Douglas Barr. Died 19/2/1917.
Private 210289 L Dolby. Died 7/3/1917.
Sergeant 200119 Robert Henry Batchelder. Died 4/4/1917.
Private T/200835 Alfred Foster. Died 6/4/1917.
Private T/201899 Francis G Quinn. Died 14/4/1917.
Private T/201157 Henry Goldsack. Died 11/5/1917.
Private T/200151 G H Luckhurst. Died 13/8/1917.
Regimental QMS 200013 George Hutchens. Died 12/9/1917.
Lance Corporal 200204 Frank Russell. Died 8/10/1917.
Private 203078 Albert Blackman. Died 21/12/1917.
Private 200855 Fred Wakelin. Died 2/1/1918.
Lance Corporal 200642 H T Milton. Died 20/1/1918.

Private 2089 Albert Ross Ames. Died 20/5/1918.
Private 203220 Sidney George Walter. Died 16/8/1918.
Private 200040 Walter Diddams. Died 21/9/1918.
Private 201481 S E Jemmett. Died 2/11/1918.
Private 210845 Jesse Sydney Boakes. Died 10/11/1918.
Private 20866 G M Kidman. Died 13/11/1918.
Lance Corporal A Whittington. Died 19/11/1918.
Private 201908 J Shoesmith. Died 29/11/1918.
Lance Corporal 200120 C L Beer. Died 13/4/1919.
Sergeant Frederick John Hutt. Died 30/4/19.
Private 202238 J H Barling. Died 16/6/1919.
Private 204361 Cyril Albert Winter. Died 16/6/1919.
Private G/20884 Bertie Charles James Dennish. Died 19/6/1919.
Sergeant 200180 S G Hayward. Died 6/7/1919.
Private 210243 S A Whitenstall. Died 26/7/1919.
Private 201086 W Gladdish. Died 24/9/1919.
Lieutenant L V H Shorter. Died 14/11/1919.
Lance Corporal 200814 Thomas Pressley. Died 20/11/1919.
Private 2000989 C E W Savin. Died 8/4/1920.

Although each and every one of the above men has a story to tell, the one which immediately caught my eye was that relating to Private 2089 Albert Ross Ames. For a start, his father, also Albert Ross Ames, was an ex-colour sergeant in the Army. By the time Albert had enlisted for four years' service in the UK, on 15 August 1914 in Folkestone with the 1st/4th Battalion, East Kent (the Buffs) Regiment, he had already served with them for a total of 4 years and 203 days. From his enlistment on 15 August 1914, he was at home up until 28 October 1914, before sailing out to Mhow in India from Southampton, on 29 October. He remained in India until 26 July 1915. From there he went to Aden, arriving there on 5 August, where he remained until 11 October 1915, at which time he was sent back to England. He was discharged from the Army on 16 November 1915 for no longer being physically fit enough for war service. His Army pension record shows the following:

Pulmonary Tuberculosis

Originated at Aden 7 August 1915. On 20 August 1915, man was admitted to hospital with cough and fever. He states he had caught a cold on the boat coming from India. No family history, except that a brother aged 2 died of Meningitis. Result of climate exposure. Bacilli found in sputum.

Remarkably, and somewhat surprisingly, when taking in to account how and when Albert first became ill, an addendum was added to this report: 'Not a result of military service or climate.'

Thankfully common sense was applied after the report had landed on the desk of the Director General of Army Services (DGAMS), who added his thoughts to the report which, it has to be said, were not exactly fully supportive of Albert's circumstances: 'A doubtful case but maybe regarded as due to military service since declaration of war.'

Such comments on a soldier's Army pension record ultimately determined whether or not, and how much, a soldier was awarded as a pension. In the circumstances, it is incredible how dismissive the initial report was. If Albert hadn't caught a cold while serving his king as a soldier on military service, travelling on a boat from one of the hottest countries in the world, India, the chances are that he would never have contracted the cold in the first place.

After Albert's discharge from the Army, he was still required to have a military medical each year, to determine his level of fitness and whether or not he was suitably recovered to be called up for further military service. Below are the comments attached to just a few of these annual medicals:

25 March 1916. Total incapacity.

27 February 1917. Total incapacity. Should not be at work.

14 May 1917. Probably he is too far gone but it is impossible to say definitely. He should be seen by the local tuberculosis medical officer.

Albert died on 28 May 1918 at the Brompton Hospital in Fulham Road, London, as a result of the pulmonary tuberculosis. He was 31 years of age; yet another victim of the war. His parents, Albert and Blanche Ames lived at Laurel Cottage, 29 Charlotte Street, Folkestone, with their four younger children, daughters, Winnifred and Lilian, along with sons Cecil and Richard.

The other obvious story, having looked down the list of names and the dates of their deaths, was that seven of the men who all died on the same day, six of whom died of heatstroke while fighting in the desert heat of Aden near Sheikh Othman. The six men who died are:

Sergeant 504 E G Dyer.
Private 2330 W Bromley.
Private 1940 G R Brown.
Private 2234 H R De-la-Mare.
Private 2289 A Steadman.
Private 2205 R W Maslin.

There is a plaque that exists which bears the names of these men, plus a couple of others. Originally this plaque had sat in a church in Aiden, but since 2000 it has been displayed at the National Army Museum in Hospital Road, Chelsea.

So many young men who never saw their twilight years, who never got to lie with a woman, who never married and had children of their own, or grandchildren. So many lives blighted by a bloody and barbaric war that so few wanted yet which claimed so many. Young men who went off to war to serve their king and country and do their duty, but who never returned to their loved ones.

It was the Great War, a contradiction in terms if ever there was one. After four years, three months and one week, it was finally over. It was the war to end all wars, well at least it ended wars for twenty years, eight months and three weeks. Then there was the Second World War, and the Great War had to be referred to as the First World War.

So, did the Great War teach society any lessons? Did politicians and military chiefs learn anything from it? Well, as the Second World War lasted for six years and one day, you be the judge. One thing is for sure, good triumphed over evil. Those who wanted war were defeated, and the Allied nations were the victorious.

CHAPTER EIGHT

Folkestone Voluntary Aid Detachment

Voluntary Aid Detachments, or VADs as they were quite often referred to, were first formed in 1909, a combination of the Red Cross and the Order of St John. The idea was that in the case of a future war, VADs, which were made up predominantly of women, could carry out the more routine and mundane parts of nursing such as changing beds, feeding patients, cleaning, making food, or even picking up newly arrived wounded soldiers from the local railway station. This would then allow full-time professional nurses to concentrate on looking after the sick and wounded.

The system of VADs was so well prepared by the time of the First World War that there were already some 74,000 VAD members working in over 2,500 VAD units all over Great Britain. Most of those who joined were from the well-off and upper classes of society, who wanted to do their bit for the war effort. One problem for a number of them was that they had never experienced hardship before, nor had they had to face the harsh reality of the discipline of hospital life. But despite this, most coped admirably with the situation and got on well with the job in hand.

At the beginning of the First World War, the British Red Cross and the Order of St John of Jerusalem pooled their resources for the benefit of the war effort, and formed the Joint War Committee. Before the war had begun, the Red Cross had managed to acquire both buildings and

A wartime medal for VADs

equipment, as well as large numbers of staff. This allowed them to set up temporary hospitals to cater for the influx of the wounded British and Belgian soldiers who started pouring into the country in the first few weeks of the war.

The buildings that were used for this purpose varied greatly in size and in what their original usage had been. They had been church halls, town halls, schools, even houses, both large and small. Some were then selected as Auxiliary Hospitals which were then aligned with nearby Military Hospitals. Soldiers who ended up in Auxiliary Hospitals tended to be the less seriously wounded ones and those who were convalescing. The Auxiliary Hospitals gained a reputation among the troops as having quite a relaxed atmosphere about them. There tended to be a calmer, less frenetic pace of life, and the discipline was not as strict as it was at the military hospitals. Whether this was intentional is not clear, but it undoubtedly sped up the recovery process for the men who had been sent to them for treatment. Those who worked at these hospitals were a combination of local part-time volunteers on the one hand, and the full-time nurses, doctors and other medical members of staff on the other.

There were two Auxiliary Hospitals that covered the Folkestone area. These were the Manor House, which was on the Leas, and provided 108 beds, and the Bevan at Sandgate.

Other hospitals included the Canadian Military Hospital at Beachborough Park on the outskirts of Folkestone, and the Westcliffe Military Hospital that specialised in eye and ear matters. There were two Army Nursing Homes, Manor Court at 38 Manor Road which could provide forty-five beds, and York House at Cheriton Gardens, which could provide forty-two beds; both of these establishments were run by local doctors. The Royal Victoria Hospital in the town was a civilian hospital, but it did its bit for the war effort; despite losing some of its staff to the Royal Army Medical Corps, it still managed to put aside 100 of its beds for the sole use of wounded Allied servicemen. It also looked after Belgian and French refugees.

With Folkestone being the main port where wounded and sick men touched foot back on British soil, it made perfect sense for the town to have enough hospital beds to care for the more seriously wounded and those in need of urgent medical treatment, rather than making them face the added trauma of a long onward journey, one which they might not survive.

Doctor Tyson had the responsibility of liaising directly with the War Office in relation to the arrival and subsequent treatment of returning wounded soldiers at the Royal Victoria. In total 1,760 wounded British soldiers were treated at the hospital during the war years, as well as 237 Belgian soldiers and 37 Belgian refugees. On top of this, many

A wounded man being cared for

soldiers with minor injuries were treated at the hospital but were not admitted to one of the wards as patients and therefore did not appear on the official figures.

There were some from Folkestone who, for different reasons, went to work at Auxiliary hospitals as part of a VAD in other towns and cities. Some even went and worked abroad in France, Belgium and further afield. But equally so, there were also cases of people who lived in other parts of the country who came to work in the hospitals in

Folkestone. There were even cases of Belgian refugees who enlisted in VADs and worked at the Manor House Auxiliary Hospital.

The Red Cross website records that there were a total of 402 men and women who had joined a VAD and who either worked in Folkestone or who lived in the town. A full and comprehensive list of all of these names can be found on the Red Cross website. Here are just a few of them:

Edith **Adams** worked at the Bevan Hospital from 16 October to 30 November 1914. Her home was at Malling Place, West Malling. She did Nursing and General. She worked at Malling hospital from December 1914 to January 22 1919 when it closed. Edith was a member of the Kent VAD number 150.

Rosamond Constance **Amphlett** worked at the Manor Court Hospital between February 1916 and May 1918, even though her home was at Acton Hall, Stourport, Worcestershire. For her wartime service she was awarded both testimonials and Kitchener's medals from doctors. She went on to work at Hartlebury Castle Hospital for Lady Sandys. Her duties included nursing on the wards and working in the operating theatres. She was paid a wage of £20 per annum.

Mrs Kate **Reeves** was a part-time kitchen helper at Manor House Hospital from 21 October 1914 to 31 January 1919. She lived at 9 Surrender Road, Folkestone, and was a member of Kent VAD 24.

Mrs Victoria Marjoria **Adam** lived at 6 Julian Road, Folkestone, and worked as a nurse from 1 September 1917 to 1 April 1918 at the Bevan Military Hospital. She also worked as a typist and as an assistant to the dispenser and was a member of Kent VAD 36.

David William **Adams** lived at 11 Gaston Road, Folkestone. He was employed as a driver between 25 November 1918 and 5 February 1919 and was paid £1.15.0 to drive the hospital's Motor Ambulance in and around Boulogne in France. His service number was 18581. He was only 19 years of age when he began working as a VAD.

Ada Madeline **Allen** lived at 15 Morehall Avenue, Folkestone. She began working as a VAD on 18 July 1917 when she was 26 years of age and was still working on 12 May 1919. She worked at the 1st North General Military Hospital, Newcastle. On 26 March 1918 she began working at the Alexandra Military Hospital in Cosham, as a nurse. She was a part-time Ward Probationer Nurse while working at the Manor

House Hospital in Folkestone. When she worked at a Military Hospital she was full-time. She was a member of Kent VAD 26.

Miss Edith Harriet **Allen** lived at Hoby in Leicester and started working as a VAD on 4 September 1916 when she was 21 years of age. She began work at the War Hospital in Dartford, on 23 January 1917 she transferred to the 1st South General Hospital in Birmingham and on 16 April 1919 to the Dispersal Hospital in Folkestone. She was officially attached to the Leicester VAD 28 group.

Miss Gladys Rose **Allen** lived at 19 Terlingham Gardens, Folkestone. Her VAD service card showed her as being a 'searcher'. On the back of her card it intriguingly said, 'Wounded are missing'.

James Lovell **Allen** lived at 69 Sidney Street, Folkestone. He worked at Manor House Hospital. He drove convoys to the hospital and did work during air raids. He worked part-time, on an as-and-when-needed basis. He started working as a VAD in August 1914 and was still in service on 12 June 1919. He was a member of Kent VAD 9.

Miss Mabel Frances **Allen** lived at 15 Morehall Avenue, Folkestone. She began working as a VAD nurse on 18 July 1917 at the 1st Northern General Hospital in Newcastle when she was 30 years of age. She remained there until 18 February 1918. On 26 March 1918 she began working at the Alexandra Military Hospital in Cosham and was still working there on 12 May 1919. She was the sister of Ada Madeline **Allen** who lived at the same address. She was a member of Kent VAD 26.

Miss Florence **Andries** had her home address at Rue du Eretieu, Jamise, Belgium. She worked part-time as a ward helper between October 1914 and October 1915. Initially she was not permitted to work as a VAD as at the time of her original application she was working in a Belgian hospital in France. Before that she worked for a few months at the Manor House Hospital.

Madeleine **Andries**, who I can only assume was Florence's and Martha's sister, or related to Florence in some way, lived at 1 West Terrace, Folkestone. I also assume that both women were in England as refugees from Belgium, having escaped the onslaught of the invading German Army, and that they somehow made their way to Folkestone. She worked part-time in the kitchen and was a Ward Probationer at the Manor House Hospital from February 1915 until 31

January 1919. She was a member of Kent VAD 26.

Martha **Andries** also lived at 1 West Terrace, Folkestone. She worked part-time at the Manor House hospital in the kitchen and as a Ward Probationer between February 1915 and 31 January 1919. She was also a member of Kent VAD 26.

Ada **Apps** lived at 45 Brockman Road, Folkestone, and worked as a part-time kitchen helper at the Manor House Hospital. She began working there on 16 May 1916 and left on 31 January 1919. She was a member of Kent VAD 24.

Jane Marie **Argar** lived at Drydene, Hawkinge, Folkestone, and was head cook for a period of eight days between 6 and 14 November 1918. She was 50 years of age when she started working for the VAD at the American Red Cross Hospital at 24 Kensington Palace Gardens in London.

Jane Marie **Argar** lived at 196 Dover Road, Folkestone. She had worked as a cook at Shorncliffe Military Hospital between November 1917 and August 1918, and after that at the American Red Cross Hospital in Kensington Palace Gardens in London from 6 November 1918 until 19 May 1919.

Violet **Astley-Sparke** lived at the Priory, Folkestone. She had previously worked in France as an 'infirmière majeure' as part of the French Red Cross, mainly as a theatre nurse at Casualty Clearing stations. She also worked at 24 Park Street in West London, which was a hospital for British Army officers. Her VAD service card mysteriously states, 'They never worked there'.

Elizabeth **Attrew** lived at 37 St Stephen Road, Upton Park and worked as a VAD between 1 August 1915 and 30 January 1919 at Manor House in Folkestone, at the Newton Abbot VAD Hospital, and at the Auxiliary Hospital at Haddon Court in Newton Abbott, in her capacity as a professional nurse. She also worked part-time at Manor House Auxilary Hospital in Folkestone.

Mrs Josephine **Baker** lived at 11 Surrender Road, Folkestone. She was a part-time ward probationer at the Manor House Hospital between October 1914 and December 1915 and was a member of Kent VAD 26.

Miss Rosalind Mary **Baker** was a native of Rochester, living at a house called Trevine, in the Boley Hill district of the town. She did her bit for the war effort. She was a full-time nurse and worked at different locations between Christmas Eve 1915 and 21 December 1918. She worked at the Rosherville VAD Hospital in Gravesend from January 1915 for three months. From there she moved to the Bevan Military Hospital in Folkestone, where she worked from 24 December 1915 until 22 January 1916 and again between 1 August 1916 and 1 October 1916. Her next place of work was the Manor House VAD Hospital in Folkestone, where she stayed for three months, working half days between 23 January and 24 April 1916. Her last place of work as a VAD nurse was at the Red Cross Hospital at 24 Park Street, London, where she undertook full-time nursing duties from 23 December 1916 until 1 March 1917, but she had to leave there because of health reasons.

Miss Sybil **Sutcliffe** worked at Manor House VAD Hospital as a part-time hall attendant. She was a resident of Folkestone, living at 64 Pavilion Gardens, so she didn't have too far to travel to work. She began working at Manor House Hospital on 21 October 1914 and remained working there until July 1918. She was a member of Kent VAD 26.

Henrietta Marion **Greene** lived at 42 Kingsnorth Gardens, Folkestone, and worked at the Manor House VAD Hospital from October 1915 in a part-time nursing capacity, as well as helping out in the kitchen. She was a member of Kent VAD 24.

Mr Walter Basil **Banks** lived at 19 Beach Street, Folkestone. He joined the VAD on 29 September 1914 and served with them through the entire war as a part-time section leader. He was a member of Kent VAD 43.

For Jean **Banks,** home was at 3 St Albans Road, Kensington, London, and she did her bit for the war effort. Between 23 March 1916 and 22 January 1919 she worked at many different locations, usually on a part-time basis, providing cover on the wards or in hospital canteens. Her first post was in France, at the American-French Hospital in Lycée Pasteur Neuilly. She worked there between April and May 1916, but then had to return home as her husband, who was in the Army, had been wounded and sent back to England to recuperate. Her next place of work was at Chatham, where she worked with Queen Mary's Needlework Guild between 1916 and 1917 (the exact dates of working were not always accurately recorded on VAD service cards). Her third place of work took her back across the Channel to work in Dieppe at the YMCA Canteen. Although part-time, she worked for over four months throughout the year. The last location that she worked at was the Canadian Westcliffe Military Eye and Ear Specialist hospital in Folkestone, between October and December 1917. The hospital was originally opened on 20 October 1915 and remained open until 20 September 1919. During that time the hospital's commanding officers were Colonel J.D. Courtenay and Colonel S.H. Mckee. Although there are no other working locations recorded for Jean after December 1917, her VAD service card shows that she was still serving with them until 22 January 1919.

Mrs Constance **Zornlin-Jourdan** lived at 11 Christchurch Road, Folkestone. She worked for the VAD between 20 July 1916 and 8 May 1918 at the Red Cross Hospital at Diss in Norfolk as part of the Norfolk VAD 78. She worked full-time in housekeeping and as a quartermaster.

Mrs **Yunge-Bateman** lived at 15 Castle Hill Avenue, Folkestone. She worked part-time between 28 February 1917 and 1 November 1918, home-making clothes and other garments for the wounded soldiers.

Miss Eleanor **Wyles** lived at a house named Adyar, in Shorncliffe Road, Folkestone. She worked for the VAD between 25 March 1915 and 31 December 1918 and was employed as an assistant matron at the No.6 Red Cross Hospital in Paris Plage, Étaples and Tronville. She was awarded the 1915 Star, mentioned in despatches, and received the Red Cross 2nd Class Medal. Her service card made mention of the fact that she 'Did useful work in the Unit'. She spent her entire service working in France.

Robert Weatherhead **Wyborn** lived at 5 Richmond Street, Folkestone, and spent the entire war working at Manor House Hospital with the rank of private. He worked part-time, on an as-and-when-needed basis. His main job was to drive the hospital's ambulance when wounded soldiers needed to be collected from the railway station. He also helped out during air raids. He was a member of Kent VAD 9. He was a painter by way of his occupation and, with his wife Mary, he had seven children, five daughters, Ethel, Winifred, Lilian, Gladys and

Marjorie, and two sons, Horace, and Robert who was 17 when the war began.

Robert William Wyborn served in the First World War, of that there is no doubt; the problem I had with this part of the research was that there were two men with that exact name, both born in the Folkestone/Dover area and both born in 1897. This is where the importance of making sure that research is correctly carried out came into its own, because one of the men died during the war and the other one survived. I just had to make sure that the one I wrote about was the right one. This Robert William Wyborn survived the war. He was born on 25 March 1897 in Dover, and before the war he was a draper's assistant. He enlisted on 30 August 1915 and was demobbed on 24 June 1919. He had joined the Royal Navy as an able seaman.

Mr Percy **Wright** lived at 22 Russell Road in Folkestone. Between 27 October 1915 and 12 June 1919 he worked at the Bevan Hospital as a part-time orderly. His duties included the transportation of wounded soldiers from the railway station to the hospital and assisting with air raid duties. He was a member of the Kent VAD 43 at Folkestone.

The VAD section for Folkestone was designated the number 43 and was set up in September 1914. The Red Cross website records the following names as having been members of this VAD. One of the roles they were expected to carry out was to work out of Folkestone Police Station every evening in shifts and deal with street-related incidents involving soldiers, regardless of whether they were the victim or the perpetrator. A thankless pastime no matter what time of the day it was.

I doubt for one second this is a complete record of everybody who served with Folkestone VAD 43 during the First World War, so if I have missed anybody out, it has been done so unintentionally:

Mr John Edward Black, 25 Bournemouth Road.
Mr William Thomas Clements, Fernley Hotel, Guildhall Street.
Mr Herbert Vincent Croucher, 23 Dudley Road.
Mr Thomas Charles Cullen, 12 Sidney Street.
Mr Percival Charles Errey, 24 Walton Road.
Mr John Henry Fox, 20 St John's Street.
Mr Albert E Franks, 43 Cheriton Road.
Mr William John Franks, 62 Tontine Street.

Mr Percival William Froud, 62a St John's Street.
Mr Harry Henley, 29 The Bayle.
Mr Ernest J Jessup, 23 Cheriton Road.
Mr Harry Oscar Jones, 11 Trimworth Road.
Mr William Charles Marsh, 9 Radnor Park Road.
Mr Leonard William May, 50 Dover Road.
Mr John McLeod, lived in Glasgow.
Mr Cyril William Milton, 41 Harvey Street.
Mr Charles Henry Roberts, 326 Cheriton Road.
Mr George Percy Searle, Harvey Lodge, Dover Street.
Mt Jesse Spencer, 1 Princess Street.
Mr Ernest Christian Stickells, 38 Castle Hill Avenue.
Mr Thomas Edward Walmsley, 27 Victoria Road.
Mr John Walker Walton, Tower House, Manor Road.
Mr Job Watts, 12 Alexandra Gardens.
Mr Charles J F Whewell, 103 Chart Road.
Mr Ronald Jack Wild, 96 Sandgate Road.
Mr Octavius Wratten, 17 Penfold Road.
Mr Percy Wright, 22 Russell Road.

As best I can tell, the number for women members of the VAD in Folkestone was twenty-four. Here is a list of just some of those who were members of Kent VAD 24, which covered the area of Folkestone during the war, specifically the Manor House Hospital:

Miss Rosalind Mary Baker.
Miss Ivy Eileen Crookes.
Miss Mary Edith D'Oyly.
Miss Dorothy Gaskell.
Miss Henrietta Marion Greene.
Miss Marie Amelia F Hill.
Miss Florence Palmer.
Miss Mabel Veronica Pigott.
Miss Hylda Florence Seath.
Miss Alice Stocker.
Miss Beatrice Mary Worth.
Miss Jean Wright.

Unlike the men, who nearly all lived in Folkestone, most of the women who were part of VAD 24 didn't in fact come from the town. It appears that the men, although happy to be part of the VAD, did not wish to travel too far afield to do so. Female members, on the other hand, appeared to be more than happy to travel far away from their homes to do the work that was required of them, no matter where they had to go.

The Kent VAD 36 covered the Bevan Military Hospital in Sandgate, which is where elements of the Kent VAD 34 also tended to work. Some even went to serve in the Field Hospitals in France.

A VAD Nurse tending to a wounded soldier

CHAPTER NINE

Women in the War

By the end of the war some 80,000 women had officially volunteered to undertake some kind of war-related work.

Many served in the different branches of nursing. There was the Queen Alexandra's Imperial Military Nursing Service (QAIMNS). It had existed since the times of Florence Nightingale, but did not receive the Royal Warrant until 1902.

The First Aid Nursing Yeomanry (FANY) was formed in 1907 and is still a charity today, with its members being volunteers. The word Yeomanry is in the title because originally they did their role on horseback. They were a link between the front lines and nearby field hospitals. Having located a wounded soldier, they would administer first aid, and then remove him from the battlefield. The FANY are not a part of the British Army.

The Women's Army Auxiliary Corps (WAAC), also known as Queen Mary's Army Auxiliary Corps, were only in being between January 1917 and November 1918, but during that time had over 57,000 members. On 31 March 1917, fourteen members of the WAAC were sent over to France from Folkestone as cooks and waitresses. There were four separate sections to the WAAC: cookery, clerical, mechanical and miscellaneous.

On top of this lots of women worked in munitions factories, where the work was long and strenuous and was most definitely a health hazard. They undertook so many different types of work which had previously only ever been the domain of men, but with more and more men being needed for the Western Front and beyond, women had to fill the gap back home. They also delivered the post, tended the fields, drove buses and taxis, became mechanics, to name just a few of the jobs that they did. The money was good, much better than they had earned before, but still less than what a man would be paid for doing the same job. With the work and wages came a freedom that they had not previously known, especially if their menfolk were away fighting in the war.

In part the topic of women in the war has already been covered, in the chapter on the Voluntary Aid Detachments and nursing, but the work that was carried out by women in the war was on a much wider spectrum than just nursing. Quite apart from being wives and mothers, the work they did in the First World War made women the very substance of what kept the country together on the Home Front.

The topic of uniformed policewomen had become somewhat of a prickly issue at a meeting of the Folkestone Town Council on the morning of Wednesday, 7 February 1917. Minutes of some of the Council's sub-committees were read out, one of which was the Watch Committee which had taken place on 29 January and dealt with matters appertaining to police and fire brigade matters. There was a vacancy in the Women Police, but Alderman Bishop suggesting that before making a decision on whether to fill the vacancy, they ought to have the Chief Constable's thoughts and opinions on the matter. It was clear from the tone of the discussion that not everybody was totally supportive of the idea of actually having women police. The police work they were expected to do was not punitive but preventative. The Chief Constable had made comment that the Women Police had not been so helpful to him in closing brothels and preventing prostitution as he had anticipated. To be fair to the Women Police officers, his comments had to be looked at in context, as during the previous year, before the Women Police had been taken on, there had only been a total of four 'disorderly houses' closed, and if this was all that fifty male constables could manage, the Chief Constable could surely not expect two policewomen to achieve more.

In seconding the motion, Councillor Stace said, 'I have every respect for the Chief Constable, but one could understand a certain amount of 'prejudice' on his part against the innovation. There could be no doubt that Women Police would be in every town before long.'

Councillor Pepper countered in defence of the Chief Constable: 'The fact that the Chief Constable was willing to work with any organisation for the suppression of indecency showed that there were no grounds for saying he was prejudiced. The Chief Constable was much more likely to know the conditions of the town than those irresponsible persons who only knew what he saw.'

Prostitution was an issue in Folkestone, like it was in similar-sized towns around the country during the First World War, and it did seem somewhat unfair to employ only two women police officers and expect them to clear Folkestone of prostitution overnight. This was, after all, a time of war; the town had hundreds of soldiers stationed at barracks in and around the town, with hundreds, sometimes thousands more coming into the town every day. Some women no doubt saw it as a good opportunity to earn money.

Under the Defence of the Realm Act, a woman convicted of prostitution or similar related offences could be expelled from their own town. Throughout 1916 in Folkestone, 63 women were convicted of prostitution and a further 22 were bound over or discharged on condition that they left the town. Although how many acts of prostitution had *actually* taken place is not known.

The topic of women police officers caused much debate. The Chief Constable had written a report, which included the matters of women police, prostitution and immorality, but it would appear that at the time of the Watch Committee meeting, it had not been widely circulated. One particular exchange became somewhat heated. Councillor Fagg said that he thought it was 'un-English' to suppress the report about the Women Police. The Mayor ruled that it was out or order to ask for a report that had been submitted to one of the council's officials. Councillor Kingsmill joined the debate by demanding to see the report, which he claimed was his right, and were he to be refused, he would write to the Home Secretary. The Town Clerk was of the opinion that the council did not have the right to claim a report made by a constable to the Chief Constable, and that he would be interested to hear what the Home Secretary had to say on the matter.

The two women police officers had been employed on a one-year trial and now one had left and the other had resigned. Before their departure they had submitted a report to the Chief Constable about the work they had carried out, the contents of which were included with the Chief Constable's regular report to the Watch Committee. The issue now appeared to be that some of the councillors found it unfair to be asked to vote on whether to employ more women police without first being able to have sight of the report that the two woman police officers had submitted to the Chief Constable, as well as his own report.

The Mayor brought the matter to a close by stating that he was strongly in favour of women police officers and that he felt that they should first wait to see his report before taking the matter further.

Ordinary housewives, especially those whose husbands who had left to go off and fight in the war, were occasionally criticised by certain individuals in the local press for not doing their bit. One woman in particular took umbrage at this and so penned a letter in reply, which was printed in the Saturday, 24 March, edition of the *Folkestone, Hythe, Sandgate & Cheriton Herald*:

> *Sir,*
>
> *I read with amazement the attack on our women of Folkestone charging them with indolence, etc. I live in the poorest locality, where nearly all the housewives leave home for daily employment. Under this terrible war cloud they are compelled so to do to make ends meet. In consequence they have to get up early, prepare breakfast, and start off the children for school. Mr Marsh need not leave his residence to see mothers in the dinner hour, line up their tiny tots, give them dinner and accompany them back to school on their way to work in the afternoon. After leaving a hard day's work, perhaps at the laundry, you can find them trying to mend boots or doing their own washing by candle light.*
>
> *We are told by visitors to the North Council School that this school is second to none in neat appearance and discipline. Surely this is a tribute alike to mother and teachers. And then some of us live seven days a week; we do not indulge in the extra half-hour's rest on Sunday morning. When at 9.30, we take our place by the side of our children in our respective place of worship, Mr Marsh may be sure we have been 'up and doing' hours: I am only one of*

many. 'The Herald' travels far and wide, and it is lamentable and hurtful to find such unjust references to the women of Folkestone. They have given their best, they are still giving their best; and they are doing their best.

In September 1917 a Women's War Workers Club was formed in Folkestone, at the Holy Trinity Parish room. It was open for three hours every day of the week accept Friday, between 3pm and 6pm. The club was managed by the same committee which made the Pioneer Club such a success. It included such luminaries as Lady Falmouth, who was the president, Lady Cohen, the Honourable Mrs Howard, and Mrs Napier-Stuart. The club catered for members of the Women's Legion and the Women's Army Auxiliary Corps who were working among the troops in the district. They were stenographers, clerks, cooks, chauffeurs, and waitresses, to name but a few occupations.

The first social event held by the new club took place on Saturday, 8 September 1917, and was very well attended. Many of the women helped to serve tea, arranged sporting events and even provided musical entertainment. Canon Gardiner lent the vicarage gardens for the event, and a heartfelt welcome was extended to all of the guests by Mrs Gardiner. It was hoped that the event would encourage lots of women to join the club.

The idea of the club was to provide a sort of respite from the hectic and somewhat chaotic working lives a lot of the women lived on a day to day basis. It was somewhere they could go to write letters, meet friends and have a cup of tea. When the weather allowed, such pastimes as tennis were encouraged. There was a needlework class, a gymnastics class, and a needlework class. On Sundays there was a bible class which was immediately followed by a sit-down tea and social hour. The highlight of the week, for some, was Saturday; this was an open day for the women to bring along their men friends. There was a membership fee that had to be paid by those who wanted to join the club, which was either 3d a week or 2s 6d for three months, which for most was money well spent.

A letter appeared in the *Folkestone, Hythe, Sandgate & Cheriton Herald* dated Saturday, 22 September 1917. It had been received by the Mayor, Sir Stephen Penfold, and had been sent from the Women's

Legion in the hope that he might be able to arrange to have it published in the local newspaper, he duly obliged:

> *It is not generally known by the people of Folkestone, what kind of work the khaki girls do, and they are the subjects of some very rude remarks made in their hearing, such as, 'What are they? A good hard day's work would do them good.' At first we decided to treat it all with the contempt it deserves, but in justice to the girls, we think it only right, to let people know that we do know what hard work is.. Would those people, we wonder, like getting up, as we do, a good four hours before breakfast which is 8 am. Our work is cooking for the Tommies, and of all of our war work, the work of military cooking is the most strenuous. Still we are happy in it, and in the thought that we are able to do this for the boys. At whatever time we go on duty in the morning, we work until 1.30pm, when another lot of girls are ready to take our place.*
>
> *This we think will show how wrong it is to draw conclusions, until the actual truth be known. But it is hard to be jeered at.*
>
> *From the W L Khaki Girls.*

The Women's Legion had been formed in July 1915 by the Marchioness of Londonderry, who was also their first commandant. They were originally based in Dartford, Kent and went on to become the largest entirely voluntary body during the First World War. Although nearly all of the work they did was for the Army, they did not come under the Army's control or that of the Government, but they were a great success all the same.

By February 1917 the Women's Legion had some 7,000 members, who were either cooks or waitresses. It was at this time that they were transferred into the Women's Army Auxiliary Corps.

During October of 1917 the Women's Army Auxiliary Corps undertook a massive recruitment drive on a national level. The idea was to have 40,000 strong and energetic

Recruitment Poster for the WAAC

women enlist before the end of 1917. They were needed to undertake all kinds of non-combatant roles for the Army, either in the base camps throughout the United Kingdom or abroad.

If accepted, women had to agree to enrol for the duration of the war, but they could choose whether they worked purely in England or whether they were prepared for service overseas. The age for the latter was 20, but if working at home, then the age was 18. A khaki uniform was provided and if a woman was assigned to work at a camp or barracks near to where she lived, then she could live at home; otherwise she had to live in hostels or billets. The main area for which women were wanted was cooking, or kitchen-related work. After that there was a need for women clerks, so that soldiers could be released from this type of work to go and fight at the front. Before the war, secretarial work, which today is a role predominantly carried out by women, was a man's job. Shorthand typists were in particular demand. Bakers were wanted, as were messengers, warehouse workers, and driver mechanics for both cars and lorries.

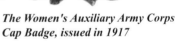

Full details locally of all of the different types of work available, the numbers of individuals required for each role, rates of pay and conditions of service, and all other particulars, were available at the Employment Exchange, 32 Tontine Street.

The Women's Auxiliary Army Corps Cap Badge, issued in 1917

Mrs Hilda M. Stainer, who was the honorary secretary of the local Pioneer Club, wrote a letter which appeared in the Saturday, 22 December 1917, edition of the *Folkestone, Hythe, Sandgate & Cheriton Herald*, on the issue of Women's Auxiliary Army Corps:

Sir,

Probably your readers are all aware of the presence in our town of large numbers of the Women's Auxiliary Army Corps, but many are not informed as to the conditions of their stay among us. The greater proportion spend about a fortnight in Folkestone, during which time they are inoculated and fitted out for their destination overseas.

It is very important that everything possible should be done to secure the highest welfare of these girls, who have accepted a heavy responsibility of service to the country. The Committee of the Pioneer Club (YMCA) and other friends are arranging for a series of concerts, lectures and entertainments to be given in the Hotel Metropole in the evening, when the members of the WAAC are at leisure but not free to leave their quarters.

I have the pleasing duty of collecting and arranging a small library for their recreation room. May I appeal to your readers to send readable books of every description to the Hotel Metropole, addressed to Miss Stevenson, for the WAAC Library. I should add that the Corps comprises over a score of different kinds of workers, with varied mental tastes.

Hoping for a generous response to this appeal.

Hilda M Stainer
Hon. Sec, Pioneer Club, YMCA.

In February 1918 an unusual matter came before the magistrates at Seabrook Police Court. Margaret Elizabeth Leecock was charged with being an absentee from the Woman's Army Auxiliary Corps without lawful excuse and contrary to the Defence of the Realm Regulations.

When challenged at her lodgings at Sandgate by Detective Constable Jacobs, she freely admitted who she was and what she had done. He then escorted her to Seabrook Police Station.

Mr E. Garnet Man, the Chairman of the Bench, enquired of Miss Leecock what she had to say for herself. She handed him a piece of paper which transpired to be a wedding certificate. Mr Garnet Man said, 'So you took French leave as they say, and got married?'

Miss Leecock replied, 'Yes sir.'

She then went on to explain that she had joined the WAAC as a higher grade clerk and had assumed because of her level of education that she would be given a comparable position commensurate to her level of intelligence, but that was not how things turned out. Instead she was made a general clerk at the Hotel Metropole in Folkestone.

The commander of the town's WAAC was in need of a secretary, and *Mrs* Leecock took the position on the understanding that she would remain permanently in that position. A new commander took over the position and she was ordered to prepare herself for service in France. She refused to go and walked out. She was given one day's leave but never returned. It was discovered that she had been visiting Corporal George Leecock at Moore Barracks.

It was WAAC procedure that if a member was absent for three days without leave, then the matter was placed in the hands of the civilian police. The WAAC member of staff who was present in court pointed out that Leecock had signed on for twelve months and had known the regulations perfectly well.

Corporal George Leecock, who was present in the court on a special pass granted through the police, confirmed that they had in fact married on 4 October 1917.

The chairman pointed out that under the Defence of the Realm Regulation Mrs Leecock had left herself liable to a fine of £100 and six months' imprisonment, but the bench had no desire to deal with her that harshly. She was fined ten shillings on the understanding that she

Relaxing outside the Metropole Hotel

went back to her allocated hostel so that the WAAC authorities could hopefully discharge her. After speaking with her husband, she agreed to return to the Hotel Metropole, and the WAAC representative was asked by the court to do what she could in order that Mrs Leecock might receive her discharge, which she agreed to do, with the support of a written copy of the court's decision and recommendations, in the hope that this would prove beneficial in achieving the desired outcome.

CHAPTER TEN

The Aftermath of the War

After four years, three months and one week of bloody and barbaric fighting, the war was finally over. Figures from the War Office, as recorded at the time, show a total of 5,704,416 men were mobilized for war. There were 734,697 men, from both the British Army and Royal Navy, who either died or were missing in action. A total of 1,668,570 Army and Navy personnel were wounded, of which 240,000 suffered either a partial or total amputation of at least one of their arms or legs.

Of those who died, 578 of them were from Folkestone.

Less than a week after the end of the war and at the beginning of the new Mayor's tenure, Councillor Huntley, of Folkestone Council, thought it was a suitable time to celebrate the fact that hostilities had ended and they all hoped that their chairman during his year of office would have the pleasure of declaring peace, for all those present felt that it was now a settled thing. The meeting had an agenda where other aspects of the day-to-day life of Folkestone needed some discussion. But the chairman said that before considering any other points or questions, he felt that the council should take the first opportunity to attend a service at the Parish Church, for although they were all grateful for the fighting efforts of the men at the front, there was a greater power which assisted them and helped them win a great victory. The chairman said that it was a most remarkable fact that from the time the British and Allied troops had recaptured the Holy Land, there had not been one single reverse. Right up until that time, there were repeated

German counter-attacks, but since the taking of the Holy Land, British troops had not been driven back one single yard.

It was agreed by those at the meeting that the chairman should visit the parish priest and arrange for a parade and a memorial service to commemorate the men from Folkestone who had lost their lives in the Great War. It was also decided that the town surveyor would be instructed to come up with a design for a bronze memorial to those men from Sandgate who had fallen in the war, which would then be placed at the Chichester Hall.

What was eventually unveiled in Sandgate High Street on 11 March 1921 was a lot grander than had at first been envisaged. The Sandgate War Memorial is a granite obelisk with a small cross sitting on top. There are brass plaques adorning each side, which include an inscription and the names of forty-six young men from Sandgate who lost their lives during the course of the First World War, including that of William Cotter VC. The inscription reads:

This cross
was erected by
public subscription
in memory of those
inhabitants of Sandgate
who fell during the
Great War of 1914-18.
It also marks the spot
where a bomb exploded
during the German
air-raid of
May 25th 1917.

Now the war was finally over, people had great expectations of a new and exciting tomorrow, nobody wanting their efforts and sacrifices to have been for nothing. Life had, and would, continue to change in many different ways.

The German Empire was the biggest loser, with the end of the war bringing to an end its forty-seven-year existence. It was one of the great powers of the day and at the start of the war it had the world's strongest Army. Russia's ruling royal family had been ousted in a revolution which ultimately cost all of them their lives. A way of life lost for ever. The Empire of Austria-Hungary had lasted for fifty-one years, until it too collapsed with the end of the First World War. It had gone from being one of the world's greatest powers to being non-existent. The Ottoman Empire, or the Turkish Empire, had been in existence for over six hundred years, first coming to prominence in 1299. The end of the First World War wasn't its ultimate downfall, but it only survived for five more years after the war ended. France was left traumatised by the war. Most of the fighting on the Western Front took place on French soil. A lot of her countryside was destroyed, as were many of her villages and towns. She lost over one million of her men killed, meaning that France had the highest casualty rate, as a proportion of the number of men who were mobilized, of any of the war's major participants.

The French Government had to spend a great deal of money, which after four and a half years of bloody war, it could ill afford, looking after millions of wounded men, which included large numbers of amputees and those suffering with shell shock. In the years following the war the country's birth rate plummeted and thousands upon thousands of children were left as orphans.

Having said all of that, the end of the war and the start of the peace was something of a contradictory time. On the one hand there would be great rejoicing in the streets that the bloodshed and the senseless loss of life had finally come to an end, but this would be tempered by the sorrow experienced by those who had lost friends, colleagues and loved ones; for them, there would be little room for celebrating.

So it was in that frame of mind that the people of Folkestone heard that the armistice had been signed. There was no elaborate ceremony marking the historic event. That would come later. For many, it would have been a time of contemplation and reflection.

Sirens could be heard all over the town as those at the Town Hall, the Harbour, the Public Baths and the Electricity Works, all sounded at once. Flags suddenly appeared in windows. This was it – the war was actually, really over, and people could celebrate like they hadn't done in years. Not only was the war over but Britain and her allies were the victors. The feeling of the war being over and having lost was an experience that only Germany and her allies had to endure.

The reassuring sounds of church bells could be heard as the belfry of the Parish Church came alive. The vicar, Reverend Tindall, gave a brief and almost spontaneous thanksgiving service. The congregation and a hastily gathered choir sang a version of the *Te Deum* and after the service, the *National Anthem* was sung loud and clear, with passion in hearts and tears in eyes, followed by a rendition of *Hallelujah*.

In places of work people simply downed tools and walked out, regardless of what their employers or foremen had to say on the matter. Formality went out the window as total strangers hugged each other, which wasn't the done thing in polite British society, but who cared, after all it wasn't everyday a war ended. The taste of victory was sweet. Even the mild afternoon rain didn't manage to dampen spirits or the enthusiasm of the moment. It was a multi-national celebration with British, Belgians and Canadians entwined as one. The band of the Buffs volunteers suddenly appeared, under the leadership of Bandmaster J. Hopkin, and the music began, patriotic sounds and favourites which everybody instinctively knew – well, not the Canadians and Belgians of course. A procession of fisherman bearing torches and headed by the Fisher Boys Band was a notable spectacle of the evening's celebrations. Everybody was joining in.

It had been many a year since so many people had cause to gather in such numbers and celebrate in such a manner. Young, old, men, women, children, civilians, military personnel, even family pets had turned the streets of Folkestone into a mass arena of celebration. It was instinctive, unplanned, natural and passionate; not a pre-planned, choreographed, official event, that more often than not ends up being more about the dignitaries than the people.

Councillor Forsyth tried his best to address the crowds from Sherwood's restaurant but the noise nearly drowned out what he had to say. He reminded everybody that the day was a great one that they were celebrating but that in the midst of their rejoicing it would be well for them to remember the heroes who had fallen and those who were still at the front. They should remember as well the wives and children, and see to it that they were looked after.

As evening approached and with the public lights having been cleaned – well, as many as was possible in the time available – the celebrations continued. There was a donkey; there was a troupe of red

Indians in colourful dress; the Salvation Army Band marched through the streets of the town playing *Men of Harlech* and *God save the Land for the People*. A large crowd of people followed on behind them, not knowing or caring where they were going. The band eventually came to a halt at the Harbour Street end of Tontine Street, the very street which had experienced the worst that Germany had to offer only eighteen months before.

The celebrations carried on across the town of Folkestone and its surrounding districts throughout the night and all of it with good humour and joy. They continued for the rest of the week, too many to record on these pages. Suffice to say, the wartime restrictions on men in uniform not being allowed into certain 'places of amusement' were cancelled, and at nearly every celebration, official or otherwise, an effigy of the Kaiser was set on fire.

A special watchnight service was held at the Tontine Street Congregational Church on the evening of 11 November to mark, as the Reverend Henry Cooper said, 'the passing of the closing hour of the greatest day in history'. A large crowd had gathered, some were from the Church's normal congregation and others who were simply passing by joined in. There were soldiers, members of the WAAC, and civilians, all there to unite in a common cause of celebration and remembrance for all of those lost in the war. In Folkestone, nowhere was that more poignant than in Tontine Street.

To end on, the following piece I believe is most relevant. They are the words of Dr John Charles Carlile, the man who wrote the book *Folkestone During the War (1914-1919), A Record of the Town's Life and Work*. He said them on the evening of the signing of the Armistice, at an evening service in the town's Baptist Church:

Now the perils of peace must be faced. They would be great, but the good spirit and sound common sense of the people would not fail. They must put the good of the whole before the advantage of any cases or section and create with the Divine blessing a new social order in which useless wealth and abject poverty would be remembered only as conditions of the dead past. Nothing was too good for our wonderful boys, but they must not be exploited in the interest of amateur politicians. They raised their song of thanksgiving and faced the future with a smile.

Sources

ancestry.co.uk

anorak.co.uk

britishnewspaperarchive.co.uk

cwgc.co.uk

Dover & Folkestone During the Great War, Michael & Christine George.

Folkestone During the War (1914-1919), A Record of the Town's Life and Work, John Charles Carlile.

kentvad.com

naval-history.net

redcross.org.uk

scarletfinders.com

Wikipedia

Index